FULFILLED

Making Peace With Our Turbulent Lives

DR. PERCIVAL RICKETTS

Copyright © 2022 by Dr. Percival Ricketts
First Paperback Edition

All rights reserved. No part of this publication may be reproduced, distributed, or transmitted in any form or by any means, including photocopying, recording, or other electronic or mechanical methods, without the prior written permission of the publisher, except in the case of brief quotations embodied in critical reviews and certain other noncommercial uses permitted by copyright law. For permission requests, write to the publisher, addressed "Attention: Permissions Coordinator," at the address below.

Some names, businesses, places, events, locales, incidents, and identifying details inside this book have been changed to protect the privacy of individuals.

Published by Freiling Publishing,
a division of Freiling Agency, LLC.

P.O. Box 1264
Warrenton, VA 20188

www.FreilingPublishing.com

PB ISBN: 978-1-956267-59-4
e-Book ISBN: 978-1-956267-60-0

Printed in the United States of America

For information address:
Dr. Percival G. Ricketts, LMHC, PA.
10031 Pines Boulevard, Suite 242

Pembroke Pines, Fl 33024

Contents

Introduction v
1   Who Are You? 1
2   Why Are You Here? 39
3   The Role of Parents 71
4   Living a Fulfilling Life 111
5   What Matters in the End 131
Final Thoughts 169
References 173

Introduction

WHO AM I? Why am I here? What am I supposed to do? Why is life so hard for so many people, including me? Why is there so much suffering in the world, so much evil? Is this all there is? Am I missing something? I must be. We are born, we grow older, daily, we experience hardships, illnesses, suffering, and then we die. What kind of a "Grand Design" is this? It just does not seem to make sense.

These, and countless other existential concerns, have been plaguing human beings forever. And, unless you are one of those individuals, who feels very strongly that some questions should never be asked, it is quite possible that you have pondered at least some of those questions at some point, perhaps even on several occasions. There is also a fair degree of certainty that you, like numerous others, have yet to find reasonable answers or plausible explanations that come close to satisfying such curiosities.

What has emerged over time, because of those unanswered, but still very relevant, and anxiety-provoking questions, is a plethora of speculative ideas about the origins of life, about the nature of our world, and about the creatures that inhabit it. Additionally, much attention has been drawn to various ideas about our perceived purpose for being here, and to the responsibilities that we have to ourselves, to one another, and to the planet on which we live. Whether we go to Heaven, Nirvana, Paradise, or Hell, there are also diverse perspectives regarding what happens after our inescapable and indomitable demise.

Some individuals feel that they know with certainty what the true answers are to most of life's difficult questions (fundamentalists and dogmatists, for example) and, some are willing to defend their positions very zealously. There are others, also, whose approaches to those matters are more guarded (the agnostics). Then there are still others, who seem to be increasing in numbers lately, who view existential matters with skepticism (some atheists, for example).

Even so, many individuals express a high degree of disdain for things that are viewed by others from a religious perspective. They prefer to use the word "spiritual," instead, because they feel it more aptly reflects how they think, and the ideas that they prefer to embrace. They do not wish to be placed in positions in which they could be viewed as conforming to organized historical principles, which they feel are outdated. They feel they are just not relevant in today's world.

The bottom-line, however, is that the search for answers persists. And, when it comes to understanding who we are, why we are here and what happens after we exit, we are in no better positions today than previous generations were. Hence, as the search continues, we hope that we will find not just the answers that we seek, but also a place where we can find peace, and perhaps-even a more comfortable understanding of ourselves.

What seems abundantly clear, is that at the root of the problem lies a great deal of confusion. The truth is that many of us, humans, are deficient in self-knowledge and self-understanding, and those two deficiencies play major roles in our ability to self-regulate and to treat each other with the consistent empathy and respect that our survival demands. Clearly, as a civilized society, we have made significant strides. Still, attention is needed not just in terms of understanding ourselves, but also in understanding the necessary steps that we need to take if we are to develop further, and if we are to attain greater self-efficacy as the most advanced species on the planet.

Many individuals, who used to align themselves with one form of organized religious system or another, are now embracing the idea that none comes close in terms of meeting their spiritual needs. Others have gone as far as expressing the view that rather than helping to meet the needs of society, and especially those who are most vulnerable, some organized religions have been preying on the poor and the needy. In some cases, some religious organizations have been implicated among the causes of a great deal of discord, division, and strife in the world.

In fact, even within some religions, a great deal of division exists. In Christianity, for example, some people feel there are too many denominations. Rather than working cohesively to promote a common cause, there are concerns that they criticize each other too much. They have not been able to agree on even some of the basic aspects of the religion of which they are all a part. This situation has been viewed as scaring individuals away, and for making potential congregants less interested in exploring the teachings more closely.

Obviously, if the main organized religious systems that have been in place (all for more than millenia), are being viewed negatively, then major overhaul might be necessary. Even so, let's face it, although religion has been

Introduction

criticized for its shortcomings, there is no denying that it promotes a great deal of good as well. Notwithstanding, many areas have been highlighted as requiring refinement. But changes may not be as easy to implement as they seem. In fact, any attempt to make significant changes to old systems, must be expected to be met with strong opposition. Many older gatekeepers of the various religions just will not allow changes to be made.

Older individuals feel that the organized systems that they embrace are just fine, and they refuse to entertain any dialog regarding reform. The burden, therefore, lies on the shoulders of younger individuals, many of whom have already been making their feelings known, and they have been staying away from religious institutions and refusing to pay any attention to what they proclaim.

Rather than trying harder to find ways to work together, both the young and the more seasoned continue to criticize each other. Older ones are criticized for failing to view things from the perspectives of younger ones. They have also been criticized for being too willing to blame younger ones when things go wrong, for accusing them of wanting to institute changes that are unpopular, and for viewing them as troublemakers who, in many cases, would prefer to discard timeless ideas rather than preserve them.

But many older folks do view younger ones negatively. They describe them, using words such as rude, disrespectful, rebellious, and contentious. They have been accused of being too self-centered, too entitled, lacking self-knowledge, and being avid seekers of instant gratification. They are seen as non-conformists and non-traditionalists, who are intent on dismantling and replacing, rather than building on the foundations that have been laid for their benefit.

Negative views of young people have not been very helpful. In fact, there are those who feel that in many cases, older generations are themselves responsible for the way things are in the world today. Rather than taking responsibility for their actions or inactions, however, they are often viewed as supposedly feeling more comfortable casting blame on the younger generations.

Many individuals in younger generations are fighting back. They feel older folks need to stop talking about the current dismal situation with young people and accept at least some of the blame. Insofar as religion is concerned, some individuals seem to share the belief that everyone, young and old, should be more ready to relinquish ideas

Introduction

that they have about religious reform or even considering other religions. They feel they should be more willing to accept old doctrines and conform to them.

Others, however, are more genuinely concerned about the state of the world, about the generational divide, and about the inability of various groups to work well with each other for a common good. They would like to see more older people mentoring younger ones, listening to what they have to say, and working with them and the fresh ideas that they often bring. They feel this type of collaborative approach would help to solve not just religious challenges, but also many others that exist.

Still, while arguably there could be some truth to at least some aspects of how older folks feel about young people today, it is not fair to make overly broad and negative criticisms of younger people as a group. After all, young people belong to a very diverse group, and those criticisms do not apply to some of them at all.

Young people do bring fresh ideas to various sectors of our society. Surely, they may be more willing to reject certain aspects of traditional life, like, for example, discarding the formal jacket-and-tie culture that many older business folks embrace, and they might be more likely to adorn themselves in more practical and easy-going shorts, t-shirt, sweatpants, and sneakers attire. In the end, however, many even in older generations seem to agree that if comfort is backed up by fresh ideas and productivity then factors like attire may not be too relevant.

Let's be fair, many younger people have played only a minor role, when it comes to how things are today, and the directions in which we seem to be heading. They have just not been around long enough. Whether we want to accept it or not, much of the credit for the very poor state of the world should well-deservedly go to members of the older generations. They are the ones who have done a very shoddy job, and they have left a legacy that is all too messy for their children and grandchildren to clean up.

Furthermore, if there is any truth to the old saying that "if learning has not taken place, it is because teaching has not taken place," then, arguably, if young people are disinterested in tradition and history and they lack self-knowledge, it must be because previous generations failed to find ways to ensure that they were more fully equipped with the knowledge that they would have required to attain a far more desirable state.

Let's not assume also that everyone in previous generations is so versed on self-knowledge, or that because

Introduction

they benefited from exposure to history and tradition, it somehow makes them more superior to their younger and less knowledgeable descendants. The reality is that the world is in a bad state and all of us, young and old, have a moral responsibility to stop criticizing each other and work together to resolve the challenges that we face.

For us to accomplish that task, it is imperative that we start with ourselves and in our own communities. It is time for us to stop setting lofty goals, which seem to suggest that attaining world peace overnight is still possible. Instead, it might be more beneficial for us to start by caring about ourselves and about each other, and for us to be more determined to make self-knowledge, self-understanding, and self-improvement more of a priority.

Yet, we still face hindrances on other fronts. Even in the new millennium, there is a great deal of poverty, hatred, and racism in the world. Not to mention the counter-productive role that politics continues to play in the inability of the world's nations to care deeply for each other, and to work cooperatively together to create a better environment for all people.

My primary reason for authoring this book is to help at least some individuals become more self-aware by encouraging them to be more introspective and to seek answers to the hard questions that have been plaguing us for millenia. This could help them find ways to uncover their own self-knowledge, to make changes that are desirable, and to think of ways to help themselves and others.

I am a Psychotherapist—a practitioner of the healing arts. During the past twenty-five years, I have had the opportunity and the honor of interacting with tens of thousands of individuals of diverse backgrounds. Most of them have sought help for their own self-improvement, primarily because they recognize that they are stuck. To thrive, they must become unstuck and sometimes they require assistance.

Of course, it would not have been possible for me to help others, without benefitting myself from the interactions with them. Many individuals have been courageous enough to willingly seek help, even at the risk of giving someone else a peek into their private world. One thing I uncovered some years ago is that helping is a symbiotic relationship. Each time the helper extends himself or herself, he or she derives significant psychological benefits also.

Certainly, I am the first to admit that I have experienced my fair share of personal challenges, and that

Introduction

I have also received help. In some cases, the challenges that I faced, have been far more complicated than those of many individuals that I have served. Yet, I have made successful transitions through the difficulties that I faced, and I am grateful for the opportunity to help others do likewise.

We are all human beings, and we face many of the same struggles. When we help others, it takes the focus off ourselves. It gives us the opportunity to share our knowledge and our expertise, while learning from others, whose experiences are much different from our own. Those interactions give us exposure to broader perspectives, from which we can help a wider cross-section of people.

Lately, I have had the opportunity to spend a great deal of time reflecting on my own journey, and on some of the unimaginable bumps that I have encountered at various points along the way. I think the pandemic has given many of us the opportunity to accomplish that. One thing that I have come to realize, it is truly all about the lessons to which we have been exposed and how we use them, both to help ourselves and to help others.

I have come to respect the resilience and the determination of the human spirit, and our ability to triumph over some of the most unimaginable adversities. I know myself much better now, and I understand who I am a whole lot better. I am more comfortable with myself and with others now, and I also realize how much of a champion survivor I, like many others who shared their various stories with me have been.

Although not always, I have tried to give the world my best at every stage, and today, I believe this is the best version of myself. I am pleased with the person, who I have been becoming, how I have chosen to live my life, and how I continue to treat others.

I am one of those individuals, who have been fortunate to be a descendant of very large families on both my maternal and paternal sides. My mother had eleven brothers and two sisters, and my father had eight brothers and seven sisters. I have survived the loss of my great grandparents, my grandparents, my parents, my nineteen uncles and nine aunts, seven of my eight siblings and many other close relatives and dearest friends. Many individuals, who are from small families, find it incomprehensible to think about how I could have adjusted to so many losses.

And yet, I have encountered more challenges in other areas of my life as well, although talking about

Introduction

them has been a recent decision. Now that I am in the fourth quarter of my life, I find myself being more vocal—sharing more about myself and who I am. I think it is important. After all, if not now, when? I have been battling a very rare illness for a few years now, and it has landed me in the emergency room a few more times than I cared for. Then, as I was in the process of writing this volume, my primary care physician, who had been caring for me for years, suddenly died. I am also a survivor of divorce after a thirty-one-year relationship. And, I have experienced parental alienation.

As psychotherapists, although we are aware of the importance of self-care, and self-regulation, we have the tendency to spend a great deal of time caring for others, while not leaving enough time to care for ourselves. Everything must begin with self. Therefore, that tendency to be consistently other-person-centered, is simply not a very good idea in the end. The advent of the pandemic and the increased demand for help-seeking and for helpers, has highlighted the necessity for many of us to work more wisely to prevent burnout. Unfortunately, this has resulted in a mental health crisis, which involves long waiting times and some individuals having to resort to utilizing their own self-help measures. These are matters that need to be addressed urgently.

Losing family members through divorce and death, epitomize the greatest challenges that human beings encounter, and even healthcare professionals including therapists are not exempt from them. One must just learn to play the hand they have been dealt to the best of their ability.

As for me, I learn not to complain and I learn never to ask, "Why me?" Even in my deepest suffering, I learn to always give my best, to focus more on those who are in more disadvantageous situations than I am, and to find peace, even during life's strongest storms.

I am a very private person. I am also an introvert. And I do not like to talk about myself. Still, I have learned how to be a "real" person, and a relatable one as well. If I am not that way now, when would be a better time?

I am grateful that I have been able to utilize the appropriate survival and coping skills to which I have been exposed throughout my professional journey, to help myself and to help others. If even one person benefits from anything that I have included in this book, it would have been well worth putting it together.

Introduction

Life is very complicated. For many individuals, each day brings new challenges. Still, we must learn how to keep ourselves afloat in this very vast, turbulent, rapids-filled stream of life. Regardless of what life throws our way, we must do our best, daily, to ensure that we remain on the positive side of the emotional spectrum. We must remind ourselves that guaranteeing our survival is paramount. No matter how difficult life gets, and no matter how hopeless it appears at times, we must find ways to rise above the challenges with which we are confronted. Giving up, or accepting defeat, are simply not options.

Many of my experiences and the challenges that I have faced, have made me a much stronger person, and a much better person than I used to be. They have also molded me into becoming a more empathetic and effective counselor. Certainly, they have not made me a perfect person. I know that no such person exists. Rather, I have become a more understanding and a much humbler one. Above all, I think I have developed a greater appreciation for the human condition, and I feel I look at life from a more mature and a more realistic perspective now.

Despite the challenges, I still consider myself fortunate, because I have never found myself in a state of disillusionment. For the first time in decades, despite the continuous buzz of background noises in this tumultuous world, I have been able to focus on the things that I believe matter, and it has helped me to find the peace that I am now experiencing. I am tremendously grateful to be still alive, and, with all its challenges and its imperfections, I have learned to love and to appreciate the life that I have.

Surely, I have lost the affection of those who died, and of others, who are no longer a part of my life. Yet, I am blessed to still have numerous friends, who genuinely care for me, who keep me grounded, and who ensure that I am never isolated. For those who continue to play a significant role in my life and in my personal growth and development, I am truly grateful.

At the stage of my life when this book is being written, I consider it a very special project for many reasons. I am much older, I am more mature in my thinking, I have seen much of the world, and I have gotten the opportunity to interact with many individuals of diverse cultures. I am a much more experienced person, and I have a better idea of what things matter. Of all the books that I have written, I am hopeful that this volume will be my best, because it could very well be my last.

Introduction

Everyone deserves to find fulfillment in their lives. And, although it often comes at a great price, everyone also deserves to find peace. Yet, living during the current pandemic, and now a war that presents reasons for all of us to be concerned, have been unimaginably challenging for many individuals, as indeed they are for me. We don't know how this will all end. But one thing we do know is that the process of life and living in these times have become even more difficult than we ever anticipated.

Many individuals find life in today's world almost unbearable at times. To those individuals, I say, "Hold on." I do not know if it was ever supposed to be easy, or that it was supposed to be easy for everyone. It certainly has not been the case for many of us. What I do understand, however, is that we possess many survival skills, and we are far more resilient than we are aware at times. We have used our survival skills successfully on numerous occasions before, when challenging situations arose. We are all survivors. We must use those skills again during these times. If they don't seem to be working, we must simply work together to develop new ones.

You may have obtained a copy of this book in various ways. Regardless of how you obtained it, however, I trust

Fulfilled

that you will get as much pleasure from reading the rest of it, as I did from writing it. Thank you.

Percival G. Ricketts
January 16, 2022

1

Who Are You?

"WHO ARE YOU?" When individuals meet, whether implicitly or explicitly; this is one of the most frequently asked questions in any language. In fact, even in situations in which the question is not asked directly, the series of questions that often follow, are usually designed to elicit deeper self-disclosure. Even in the rest of the animal kingdom, there is the tendency for animals to try to get to know each other or to satisfy their curiosities about each other during encounters.

If a person is walking their dog and they meet someone, who is doing likewise, the dogs will circle each other, sniff each other, and perform their "getting to know you" ritual, as if to say, "Who are you?" Only after that ritual is performed do they seem to attain some level of comfort, so that they can be at ease.

Meanwhile, the owners of the dogs usually do something similar. They ask each other questions about themselves and their pets. They hope the answers will provide them with further insight into who their new acquaintances are. One person may say something like, "My name is…" and then they would ask, "What's your name?" "Where are you from?" "What breed is your pet?" "Is it male or female?" "How old is he/she?" "How long have you had him/her?" If it's a male, the other person may ask, "Is he neutered?" and if it's a female, "Has she been spayed?"

In our xenophobic culture, the "Who are you?" question that is asked when people meet is not unusual. It is designed specifically to invoke mutual self-disclosure, which is quite appropriate. Let's get to know each other, so that we are no longer strangers. I am willing to tell you things about me and answer your personal questions, and I hope you are willing to do likewise. Those statements are usually implied in initial conversations.

While the answers can, and they often do provide superficial information about another person, it is still debatable, whether they really provide meaningful information that helps one individual get to "know" another. The answers do, however, satisfy some curiosities about others. But we, humans, like to keep things superficial, especially with new acquaintances. Only after we get to know someone well are we willing to divulge more information to them about ourselves.

Who Are You?

Sometimes, we also like to put the initial encounter ritual up a notch as well. If I am with a friend that you have never met, simply by being with him/her implies that when we meet you, at least a polite introduction is in order. "This is…" "He/she is…" and we say something about the person that we are with, before turning to the other person and saying, "This is…" We say something about the other person also. Then, depending on the culture and the circumstance (business, casual, ethnicity, etc.), hands might be shaken, kisses may go on one or both cheeks, or hugs may be exchanged.

Even so, we do not want to get too carried away with questions, answers, or introductions when we meet someone for the first time either. The next time someone asks you, "Who are you?", try getting into a deep philosophical or intellectual discourse about who you really are. In our fast-paced society in which time is a precious commodity, very rarely do people wish to really get to know another person. Indeed, regardless of your interpretation of the question, it is not an invitation for self-exploration or deep conversation. I assure you, in many cases, if you start sounding philosophical or intellectual when you just meet someone, it is one of the easiest ways for them to move on very quickly.

Without seeming rude or impatient, a person will probably find some way to say, "Sorry, I have to go," or "let's finish this conversation another time." Additionally, the other person will probably leave with a negative impression of you. They may even be wondering whether something is wrong with you or how they could avoid having other encounters with you in the future.

So, let's examine this "Who are you?" question more closely. When someone meets you for the first time, or they might have met you before but simply don't remember you, it is quite appropriate for them to ask the question. How you choose to answer can be crucial.

Interestingly, you may notice that the question was not, "What is your name?" Yet, many individuals usually respond with, "My name is…" And they proceed to give either their first name, their first and last name, or even their nickname, depending on the situation. Some even give their title, indicating how they prefer to be called.

In an unscientific online poll conducted in January 2022, most respondents (50 percent) indicated that when asked the "Who are you?" question, they usually respond with their first name only. Forty percent indicated that they usually respond with their first and last name, while the other 10 percent said that they are usually not sure how to respond. Interestingly, some individuals indicated that in situations they have either used the first or second response above, or they try to avoid the question altogether. Many people do not like being asked who they are or what they do.

Even so, it is almost universal for individuals to accept either a first name or a first name/last name combination as an appropriate response to the "Who are you?" question. In fact, it is not unusual for any other response to be met with confusion.

But is one's name really who one really is? Is providing one's name really an appropriate response to the "Who are you?" question. Even as unique as my name is, I met someone years ago, and he has the identical first and last names as me. Our given names are what we are called. Therefore, in this vast world with so many people, no matter how unique the name, it is not inconceivable that others could share the same names as we do. Owing to this realization, self-identifying by one's name(s) alone, can be problematic in some instances.

Many years ago, I was visiting the country of Colombia in South America. I used the opportunity to try to find an old friend, with whom I attended college at Virginia Tech, several years before. After graduation, he returned home to Colombia, and I went back to my native Jamaica. It had been many years, and we simply lost contact with each other.

As soon as I realized that I would have been visiting Colombia, I started trying to locate my friend. My search, however, always led to a dead end. Finally, while there, in a last-ditch effort to locate him, I looked for his name in the white pages of local telephone book that was in my hotel room (I would not be too surprised if some young people do not know what white or yellow pages are, or even what a phone book is). To my surprise, his name was probably one of the most common in the entire city. It was so common that it spanned almost 4 pages of the telephone book.

The point is, although it is very convenient and even a very common way to answer the "Who are you?" question, it gives responses that are both general and unreliable. It does not provide enough specific information that could enable one person to be distinguished from another. One can learn someone's name. Still, without further information about that individual, nothing else can be known. Additionally, if two or more individuals with the same names are in one location, it can result in confusion.

Who Are You?

Learning about oneself is a very complex process. How much one knows about himself/herself can also affect that individual in many ways. As a psychotherapist, I have a deep interest in people. To do my job effectively, I need a great deal of information about those whom I serve. I am intrigued by their similarities to others, by their differences, and by the behaviors that they usually display. I am also interested in how they present themselves in various situations.

Knowing my clients' names alone, will simply not suffice. Thankfully, my position affords me the opportunity to learn unique bits of information about my clients that many of their very close family members or even their best friends may never know.

Asking someone to self-disclose information that they usually keep privately, is often a very interesting exercise. Not only is it often unusual and uncomfortable for them, but also, it sometimes leads them to explore and reflect on aspects of their lives on which they probably have never ventured. They usually recognize that they are embarking on a road that will lead them to self-discovery, self-knowledge, and self-understanding, but many, quite frankly, are usually not ready to engage in that kind of exercise.

I have a deep interest in parenting matters, and particularly those that pertain to fatherhood. Interestingly, over the years, I have noticed that some individuals, who might not have been raised with their biological parents (they may have been adopted, or they may have been estranged from their parents, particularly their father), sometimes find talking about self-exploration particularly challenging. In fact, for some individuals, if it is not something that they are ready to explore voluntarily, it can make them feel rather uncomfortable.

Trying to get some individuals to discover themselves and to understand some of the factors that may have contributed significantly to their current situations, and how they view the world, is usually not without some anxiety. That type of exchange, can, and often does bring up many unusual concerns that they might not have anticipated.

The issues that sometimes emerge, lead some individuals to realize how very little they really know about themselves. Oftentimes, it also causes them to respond by saying, "That's not of interest to me," "That is not a problem for me," or "I don't find such matters important." Yet, there is the observation that, deep down, some individuals would like to explore the matter further. As many

Who Are You?

individuals get older, they sometimes recognize the importance of self-knowledge and self-understanding.

Many individuals are aware that a connection exists between their parents, their backgrounds, and their behaviors. They often agree that once that connection has been explored, and they are usually willing to make some changes, they are sometimes able to make peace with some situations and even with themselves. This is when some individuals say they usually begin to live life more meaningfully and they excel.

On the surface, getting to know oneself may not seem very interesting or even important. I have come to understand, however, that matters pertaining to subjects like self-knowledge and self-understanding, are based on personal interests and personal choices. They are not matters that are usually of interest to everyone. Therefore, very frequently, they are not willingly explored. After all, when this type of knowledge is uncovered, what is the next step in the process? How will this new information be utilized? Many individuals are uncertain. So, they sometimes find it much easier to put the matter to rest.

The truth is, if self-discovery and self-understanding cause individuals to change, what will the new person be like? How will they fit into the world to which they have grown accustomed? Perhaps the more interesting questions though, could include the following:

1. If there is no self-discovery and no change, can there still be self-growth?
2. Without self-growth, can one still attain self-efficacy and self-actualization?
3. Without this type of self-exploration, can one still find peace and happiness?

My interest in self-knowledge and self-understanding began in my early childhood when I developed an interest in my identity and my roots. The situation became especially important for me during my first exposure to genetics, when I was a teenager in public health school. It enabled me to develop an even keener interest in myself and in who I am. I started looking at certain family traits that I now think are paramount in family studies.

I examined, for example, certain generational patterns that could affect me and even my offspring. The patterns include, for example, the presence and the prevalence of both physical health and mental health conditions among my family members. Not only do I consider these very important matters, but also, where possible, I believe they should be explored by individuals before they get into serious relationships, and before they decide to marry and have children.

I recognized that there were individuals in my family on both sides, for example, who have either the Sickle-cell trait or full-blown Sickle-cell disease. I learned that in individuals of African descent, this is a very important consideration, because the presence of the trait or the disease, could signify a strong possibility that the disease could occur in children that result from a union between individuals of similar backgrounds.

The incidence of many other conditions was also researched. These conditions include diabetes, heart disease, hypertension, Alzheimer's and dementia, prostate cancer, breast cancer, depression, and anxiety. Perhaps even more importantly was the discovery that many of those conditions were either not present or they were not as prevalent in my family as they were in others. At the same time, I discovered that some conditions like hypertension, which is common in my family, are either not as common in other families, or the research may not have been done.

Of course, poor record keeping and the reliance on memory, especially with older people, can lead to unreliable information at times. Notwithstanding, what I find rather interesting also are the answers to questions, such as, "How old were great-grandparents when they died?" "How did they die?" "How about my grandparents?" "How did they die?"

I am aware of how my grandparents died, how old my father was when he died, and how he died. I identified a significant health link between my great-grandfather, my grandfather, my father, and me. I have a direct connection with all these men, and I have been able to use that knowledge to make better decisions about my own health and how I choose to live my life.

I do realize also that I am one of the luckiest persons in the world when it comes to securing information about my family. At one point, I had the luxury of having four centenarians alive in my family. When one is afforded the opportunity to spend time with family members, who are very old, the acquisition of invaluable information is possible. Old folks are a gold mine when it comes to obtaining important historical family data.

Just a few years ago, one of my father's elder brothers died at the ripe old age of 110 years. We had a very strong uncle-nephew bond, and, luckily, he enjoyed talking about himself, about the past, and about family matters. He was one of my most important family resources, when it came to family relationships and medical conditions that affect men in my family. He was a great contributor to my self-knowledge and to my self-development.

I had the opportunity to interview not only my uncle, but also many other family members who were willing to share their knowledge. I took copious notes, I made video and audio recordings, and I even developed elaborate genograms, which go back a few generations. The information I obtained from my research has greatly influenced my self-knowledge and my knowledge about my roots and I have become the self-appointed family historian.

The historical information that I obtained over the years about my family is of unquestionable importance. Still, I realize that very soon it might all be meaningless. What I have discovered is that many young people in my family today lack interest in such matters. Therefore, although the information is available now, and many individuals wish they had similar resources about their families, when I die, it could truly be the beginning of the end of that history.

So, how does one gain self-knowledge? There is no implication that one must spend time with generations of old people in one's family. Sometimes they no longer exist. In some families they either died early or that type of relationship might simply not exist.

I have some friends, who were adopted, and they have impressive self-knowledge. On the other hand, there are others, whose parents and even their grandparents are still alive, but they are either estranged or they have no significant interest in family matters. Information about one's lineage and family relationships can play major roles in one's life and in one's self-knowledge. However, it does not mean that in the absence of that information, self-knowledge and self-understanding are adversely compromised or that they are impossible to attain.

But this is not a simple matter either, especially when the interest is just not there. What I have observed also, is that many young people have neither the time nor the patience that such matters demand, to sit and listen to older people talk about family history. They are just not interested in hunting down older relatives or in asking them questions about their roots.

When it comes to self-knowledge, many unanswered questions will always remain. Still, I suggest that if this is an area of interest and older relatives are available, hunt them down and talk to them. Unfortunately, in many instances, the opportunity has been lost already due to the death of senior family members with good knowledge of family history. Simply put, when older people lose their memory or when they die, very important family information is lost.

Now that I fall among the ranks of those who are termed "senior citizens," I will use this opportunity to express my dissatisfaction with the way in which older people are treated in this country. I have been working with senior citizens in counseling for many years, and I think some of their stories of isolation, loneliness, and exploitation, after they spent the better part of their lives raising their children and their grandchildren, are just plain shameful.

In this, the most advanced country in the world, I believe it is time for us to start doing a much better job of caring for our senior citizens. There are those who, however, feel that the situation should not be so surprising, considering the changes that have unfolded over time, and how we relate to others in our society.

The situation is also expected to worsen. After all, with advances in science and medicine and our continued focus on living longer, what will happen if we continue to live longer, and we don't learn to care for each other? There will certainly be more old people in the world in the future. In fact, the senior citizen group in this country has been growing exponentially for some time now. As people's self-knowledge increases and as they continue to take better care of themselves, many individuals are expected to live much longer than their progenitors.

Throughout the years, and in all my travels, I am yet to meet someone who I could say has perfect self-knowledge or perfect self-understanding. I have, however, met many individuals, for whom one of their biggest challenges could be a lack of self-knowledge or a lack of interest in their own self-knowledge. Many are aware of their situation, but the matter is not of too much importance to them.

Some are also the ones who, when asked, "Who are you?", They answer with just their names, because it is convenient, and it is what they think is expected of them. They willingly leave it at that because they have no desire to explore the matter further. Interestingly, if they were asked about their family's background or the origin of their surname, how little they know about their roots, usually emerges as well.

How does one gain self-knowledge and self-understanding? How should one begin the journey toward self-discovery and self-development? How can one attempt to uncover who they really are? This seems simple enough. However, it can be a rather challenging undertaking and one to which many individuals have not given enough attention. As a result, self-ignorance has become a very common phenomenon in many parts of the world. It lies at the root of many of the challenges that we frequently encounter.

If, indeed, we are going to make greater strides in terms of our own understanding, then we must be willing to do more self-exploration and make the changes that are necessary for our self-development. It is true that everything starts with self. If there is a lack of self-awareness or self-understanding, how can one be expected to relate to others meaningfully? If one does not love oneself and they do not know how to treat themself well, it should be expected that how they treat others would be consistent with their self-treatment. It is a very fundamental principle, and it is crucial for our continued existence.

Before embarking on a self-discovery journey, there must first be the recognition that a lack of self-knowledge exists. One must also not only just wish to know more about oneself, but they must also have the desire to use the knowledge for their self-improvement and self-empowerment. One must first come to terms with one's own self-deficiencies, otherwise, self-discovery becomes far more challenging, and the journey might seem pointless.

Using the tools that one has at their disposal, they must be willing to do whatever it takes to uncover more information about themself. Certainly, unless one has certain intellectual deficits, there is no such thing as someone who lacks total self-knowledge. Whether others are aware of it or not, even if it's only the idea that we exist, we all possess some knowledge of ourselves. Still, there is always room for growth, room to learn much more.

Each person must become more introspective, and they must be willing to perform their own self-analysis. This is the only way to determine what is already known and what more may need to be known. This is the first step for any individual, who wishes to embark on the road toward self-discovery and to a much more desirable place in the world.

Of course, there could be those who feel that they are well-versed in self-knowledge already. So, there is no more room for improvement. For them, this exercise

Who Are You?

could lead them to a place of total surprise. For others who recognize that they have limited self-knowledge and they would like to improve, they have many resources at their disposal.

When the right resources are utilized effectively, they can help foster better self-understanding and self-development. They are not just useful tools. They can function as catalysts that propel an individual seeker of knowledge much further along the path toward self-discovery and self-improvement.

Nowadays, there appears to be renewed interest in matters of lineage and self-knowledge. Consequently, there has been a correspondingly great increase in the number of individuals who are utilizing genetic and ancestry tracing in making family connections. Almost overnight, this has become a billion-dollar industry.

Before delving into the heart of the matter, however, it is important for us to agree on some basic principles regarding "self." Against this background, without getting into any religious conversations, everyone could be conceptualized as being composed of two main components—an outside container that we can see, that we call the body, and an internal component—the content, which we never see, but we are sure it exists.

To make things simpler and clearer, similarities could be made between the content and the wind. We have never seen the wind, we only feel the breeze on our skin or see the trees sway and the leaves move. In the same way, the content that we know is inside of us directs our thoughts and our feelings and it allows our bodies to move.

The central part of this container-content connection is a physical brain that is housed in our skull. The brain is our unique computer. It is akin to a computer's Central Processing Unit (CPU) that stores intelligent information, processes it, and allows for retrieval when recall is necessary.

When the brain is damaged, or if it shuts down for any reason, the computer is out of commission, and the stored information is inaccessible. If the entity dies, which means that the brain no longer functions, all the stored information no longer exists.

Each content needs a physical, viable container to exist and to function optimally. When an individual dies, because they are the container plus the content together, and one cannot exist independently of the other, logically, it is the point at which the individual no longer exists. The containers, or our bodies, are not us. They are an essential part of us, but they are no longer viable after there is the separation or liberation of the contents that used to occupy them. Regardless of how we choose to dispose of them, containers disintegrate when they separate from their contents. We are certain of that. Without the content, a container is just a container, nothing more.

We know for sure that the invisible part of us will continue to exist if it remains embodied or containerized. However, once liberation or separation occurs at death, that's where our knowledge of ourselves as individual entities stop. No one alive knows for sure what the next step is. Call it faith, call it belief, we simply do not know.

The million-dollar question is, what happens to the content, the part of us that we never see but we know exists? What happens to the essence of us when we die? Many individuals are willing to enter pointless, robust debates about this matter, especially on religious grounds. However, no person has any more knowledge about the matter than anyone else does.

Logically, religion does have a very important role to play in this regard, because it provides hope that there is something after our container and its content separate. It enables us to live our lives a certain way, and it reinforces the idea that we don't just cease to exist at the point of death. Humans have been conditioned to think that there is something more. Looking at the world with its order and how things function also provides reasonable evidence of significant and timeless existence. Yet, we see people die daily, and we have no good understanding of what happens after their death. No one has ever returned after they die. We simply have never witnessed that. Therefore, in the absence of any evidence, it is very difficult to affirm that anything lies beyond, unless it is on religious grounds, on which faith is involved.

Even so, we, human beings, are not willing to face the impermanence of a significant existence to which we have become accustomed. Despite ubiquitous evidence to the contrary, somehow, it appears that some of us still feel that we will be among the ones who cheat death, who will continue to live. We somehow feel that it may never happen to us. As if we think, somehow, it could happen sooner if we thought about it—there are some among us who refuse to give it any thought whatsoever.

If we only take better care of ourselves, we think, if we exercise more frequently, if we get adequate sleep and do good deeds. Perhaps we are going to be around forever, or we may even find ourselves in another place

Who Are You?

that is much better afterwards. We feel we are going to find our rightful place among the immortal, because we did so much good, or because we lived by a particular unverifiable script. But none of that has been proven to be true yet.

As we grow older, it is not unusual for us to start a countdown of the possible time that we think we may have left. Some of us even get into a state of panic. Oh, where did the time go? Has it been seventy years already? If only we had more time. There are so many things we would probably have done or done differently. Then, when we hear of our peers or even younger ones dying, it becomes more anxiety-provoking for us.

To secure a few last-minute pats on the back, some people may start doing good things as if that will somehow erase years that were spent doing bad things. They may start embracing religion, especially seeing it promises forgiveness of sins, regardless of how long those sins were committed or how egregious they might have been.

The wealthy may start giving away their money. After all, if there is an afterlife, there is no known use of currency there. Many individuals come to realize that regardless of how much wealth they may have accumulated here, they simply cannot take it with them. They dole out scholarships and good wishes. They say things like "God bless you." or "I love you." They start noticing the homeless and the poor.

They start attending religious institutions and they might start tithing handsomely. They develop bucket lists. Some even pay off other people's debts or they may give away cash to unsuspecting and grateful strangers. They want to do things that they feel are important, things that they feel suddenly matter.

Especially if they are facing health and other challenges in later years, some individuals start to engage in behaviors that others find admirable. They replace partying with hymn singing and praying. They become more repentant and more accessible to others. They visit the sick and they find more time to spend with them. Caring for the sick, somehow reminds us of what awaits us if we survive long enough, and being around the sick, and especially the dying, provides us with reminders of our own mortality.

This is not meant to criticize others for doing as they wish with their money or with their lives. People do have the right to live and to behave as they see fit, especially if some good is involved. Furthermore, many individuals

Who Are You?

do genuinely reach out to others because they may have had their own experiences with lack and suffering in the past, and they see it as their way of giving back and of helping from the heart.

Some people who amass great fortunes build schools and provide an invaluable education to children for whom the opportunity would have been otherwise unattainable. Some are known to build health centers and hospitals to care for others in need. They provide biologics, medicines, and other essential medical resources.

Others provide potable water, food, and shelter for some of the world's most underserved. Those are some of the individuals, who remind us that despite imperfections, there is still a great deal of good in the world and there are many who have the means, and who really do care about the welfare of others.

Among the strange behaviors that some individuals exhibit in later life, include attending more funerals, particularly viewings. Some individuals find it distasteful, and they stay away, because looking at a body in a coffin makes them wonder about their own demise. They imagine themselves lying there, lifeless, while others come to stare and say kind words that they were never told when they were alive. They listen very keenly to eulogies, and they wonder what will be said about them.

Then, some individuals secretly grieve, not for the dead, but for themselves, for their own inevitable exodus. They enter a type of anticipatory grieving process, as they reflect on their own lives. They think about the things that they did, or that they failed to do, and what they should start doing now, in whatever time they think they have left. How do they find peace? Who have they wronged? With whom should they reconcile?

Some individuals get stuck here, and for that, some of the courageous often decide to seek help with professional counselors or with religious leaders. This help-seeking process gives them the opportunity to express some of their deepest feelings. It reinstills hope in them that there is still time to make changes, and it often brings them peace.

The powerful nature of religion and its role in our lives cannot be overemphasized. Not only does it provide us with a significant template on which to build our lives, but it also offers us a promise of redemption when we inevitably make mistakes or when we do bad things. Many individuals who purport to be religious find it offensive when others don't see things from their perspective. How could anyone believe anything different? How could they feel that they have the right to question written religious words?

In the name of God, some even hurt others, and they find it justifiable to do so. They feel strongly that the ideologies that they choose to embrace are the right ones and they are worth defending. They are convinced that they have been commissioned to carry out their defense, and that they will be rewarded handsomely in the hereafter, for "spreading the word," and for "converting souls."

Religion makes us feel that this life that many find so inundated with sin, evil, and suffering, is worthwhile. It makes us feel that we should be grateful to be here, and that after this life, while some are punished, perhaps even eternally for bad behaviors, others will enjoy substantial rewards for good ones.

Over 35 percent of respondents in the January 2022 unscientific poll about life indicated that when one dies, they go to a better place if good behavior is displayed here. Most individuals (over 40 percent) affirm that what happens will depend on the religion that one chooses to embrace here.

Following are some suggested activities that may be worth considering and some activities that may be helpful, if there is a desire to embark on a journey toward self-discovery:

- Recognize that this is all about you, about your personal growth and your self-development. Even so, when you improve, everyone in your circle also improves.
- You must be prepared for changes. Expect those in your circle to do one of three things—some will want to find out more about what you are doing, and they will support you. Some will criticize you because they may not understand what you are trying to accomplish. Don't be surprised if they become unsupportive and they start to slight you. Thirdly, some may blatantly choose not to be in your company anymore and they will abandon you. Do not allow that to deter you. View it as a favor. They are providing more space for you to develop.
- Concentrate your energies on yourself and on those who are understanding and supportive. When I decided to pursue doctoral level studies, even some very close family members and friends were unsupportive. I still remember some of the

comments—"You already have a master's degree, why would you want to go back to school? You are too old. A doctorate is tough, it is going to take up too much of your time. Almost 85 percent of people who start a doctorate, stop at ABD (all but dissertation). You are already making enough money. You are only doing this because you want people to call you doctor. You are only going to put yourself further in debt at this late stage of your life when you should be having fun and thinking about your retirement. I will neither be supportive of you nor your career." Let's just say, today I have my doctorate. I learned a great deal. It has enabled me to put myself in a position to help others at a level that I could not have, had I chosen to remain where I was. The bottom line is that there comes a time in your life, when you alone must make decisions about your life, even if others don't understand or they choose not to support you.

- Recognize that to get to know yourself better, you must be willing to do the work, no matter the cost. You must be willing to stay the course and be prepared to change.

- Take a self-inventory. You must know where you are, where you are starting from, and where you would like to go.
- Start by asking yourself, for example: What are some of the things that I would like to change about myself? These could be certain bad habits, negative behaviors, or emotions. Solicit the help of dear friends or close relatives if you so desire, especially if they can be objective and supportive.
- Get professional assistance and guidance from a counselor, a coach, or a mentor.
- Become more self-critical by asking yourself, for example: If I do this, how will it benefit me or others? How could changes that I make now disrupt my life and my family's functioning? Is what I am doing now the most helpful or the most productive? What could I be doing that could be more helpful? What costs (financial and emotional) could be associated with making changes to my life now? What will it cost me if I remain as I am?
- Examine your relationships with individuals in your outer circles including coworkers, friends, extended family members. Are they negative and

unsupportive toward you? Do you trust them? What can you do to make your relationship with them more positive? Is it possible for you to do so?

- Examine your relationships with individuals in your inner circle—specifically with your parents, siblings, spouse or significant other. Are any of those relationships strained? What can you do to improve them? What do you or they need to do to fix the situation? Is there unfinished business between you and anyone that needs to be addressed for growth to take place? What will be the cost emotionally or otherwise to improve those relationships or to keep them the same? If your undesirable relationship with someone does not change and the person dies, will you be okay with that?
- Start making positive changes in your life. Have you been putting off going to the doctor? Do you see the need to take better care of yourself? Stop making excuses and get yourself checked out medically and mentally. By the time symptoms show, some conditions could be advanced. If screening was done early, not only could you have

probably detected them earlier, but earlier detection may have increased your chance of having a positive outcome. But even before you decide to go on that diet to lose a few pounds or before you decide to start visiting your neighborhood fitness center more regularly, it is a good idea to get yourself checked out medically, especially if you have not done so recently, if you are predisposed to certain medical conditions, or if you have been having some symptoms already. Get a Primary Care Physician (PCP) or visit a public health clinic if you do not have health insurance and you cannot afford to pay for it privately. It is rather ironic that quite often, some of the same individuals, who will say that they cannot find the time to go to the doctor or they cannot afford the cost of healthcare, are the same ones who will travel to exotic places on expensive vacations. They pay large sums for concert tickets and even more to attend sporting and other events, on which they seem to have attached greater importance. Do not just take a one-time trip to the doctor. Your body and your mind are under constant stress, and they are constantly changing. Decide to get an annual physical examination. While you are at it, also get an annual mental health check-up. Your mental health is just as important as your physical health. You would not have had a complete health examination if it did not include a mental health examination. No matter how old you are, get to know your changing body well. Write down a list of things that need to be checked and when. If you are a woman, ask your doctor about the pap test, and mammography. If you are a man, ask about testicular self-exams for testicular cancer, and ask about prostate exams and prostate screenings. This is where knowledge of your family history could be very helpful. Do you know first-degree relatives that have certain significant medical conditions that put you at high-risk? Is there a history of certain cancers in your family? Is there a pattern, in terms of when certain conditions usually show up? How close are you to that age? How could your lifestyle put you at greater risk for certain conditions? Has there been a history of mental illness in your family on your maternal or paternal side? These are very important questions, because, according to current data from the Centers for Disease Control and Prevention (CDC), out of every four people in the United States, one has a diagnosable mental health condition, which is usually a mood disorder or an anxiety disorder. There are also strong indications that the rates of these disorders have increased since the inception of the COVID-19 pandemic.

- Reduce stress and worry in your life. Start by collecting helpful resources. Do you have "stuff" on your mind, or do you have relationship or behavioral challenges? Consult with a mental health professional. Do you have any medical concerns that are bothering you? Do you constantly have financial trouble? Decide what your needs are and those will determine the resources that you seek.
- Have you been thinking that the suffering would end or that the world would be a much better place if you were not in it? Seek professional help, talk to a trusted friend, or call the suicide hotline at 1-800-273-8255. Confidential help is available, and you do not have to continue to suffer on your own.

- Exercise—depending on your age, even brisk walking a few times weekly can be very helpful. Check with your doctor first.
- Don't be afraid to step out of your comfort zone and try new things. In addition to conventional medicine, research some alternative medicines and techniques that have been around for millenia, including Ayurveda, acupuncture, acupressure, yoga. They may complement what you have been doing already. Talk to your doctor about them as well.
- Never underestimate the power of a "good night's sleep."
- Drink "enough" water. Talk to your doctor about how much you need.
- Eat "wisely." Consult with your doctor and a nutritionist.
- Find out what things are good for you and what are not so good as you age.
- In many cases moderation is key. But don't get into moderation so much that you stop enjoying your life.
- Make a list of other questions to which you might need to find answers and start researching. Be

committed. You could get frustrated at times and other things may come up. Take a break if you feel overwhelmed but decide when you will resume. Don't give up. Look how much you have learned already.

- Recognize that no matter what you do, you will never have a perfect life, but you can have a better one.
- Develop a code that you would like to live by. Have some rules. Stick with your plan. You developed it. It is yours. Others do not have to understand everything that you do, and you have no obligation to explain it to anyone either.
- Find some way to serve others. Do something for others, especially if you know that they can never return the favor.
- Be humble
- Respect yourself and others.
- Be true to yourself. Be authentic.
- Learn to love your life. Make changes when they are necessary but learn to love yourself.
- Be polite. Learn to say little things like "Good morning," "Please," and "Thank you."

Who Are You?

- If someone means something to you, let him or her know, now.
- In challenging situations, ask yourself, "What should I do to maintain peace?"
- Look for humor in situations and at least smile. Sometimes even laugh out loud. Learn to laugh at yourself as well, especially when you are alone. Don't take yourself too seriously.
- Reflect on your life often. Learn to use your mind's eye and go back. Find positive memories and relive them. I used to tell my patients to look in the windshield often and don't pay much attention to the rearview mirror. I no longer do that. Recognize that both the windshield and the rearview mirror are essential. Ask someone with Dementia or Alzheimer's Disease how important being able to remember things would be—even some of the not so good things. Both good and bad things happened in your past. Look back at some of those good memories and recapture them.
- Learn to meditate.
- If you are religious, pray often.

- It takes courage to ask for help but it is worth it. Know when and where to find help.
- Make a few new friends. Quite often they are into the same things you are, so they are right there. If you are unable to find one, choose to become one. Don't be afraid to make a few younger friends as well. They are a source of new ideas, and they are less likely to predecease you.
- Never forget how short life is. It could be over in an instant.
- Recognize that the world is made up of unique individuals who belong to unique families they did not choose. Do not compare yourself with others. Regardless of your personal situation, start from where you are and decide what kind of person you would like to become. You can still discover yourself. You can still develop self-understanding, and you can still excel.
- Constantly improve! Grow! Live until it is your time to die! Enjoy your life!

2

Why Are You Here?

QUESTIONS REGARDING WHY humans inhabit this planet, have been at the forefront of our minds for ages. In the recent January 2022 unscientific poll about life that was conducted with adults between the ages of twenty-five and seventy-five, most respondents (40 percent) indicated that they believe they are here "to do good in the world." Approximately 30 percent suggested that they are here "to enjoy life and be happy," and 15 percent indicated that they are here "to worship God." The other 15 percent indicated that they are "not sure why they are here."

Although the participants were from diverse religious and ethnic backgrounds, the poll had many limitations. These include what their concept of God is, and how they might be worshiping Him. What do they think "doing good" means? What constitutes "happiness" and the enjoyment of life?

Those concepts could have different meanings to different people. Despite subtle differences, however, many people seem to have a basic understanding of what is being asked. Arguably, if 40 percent of any adult population is following their beliefs and they are doing good, by any measure, that is still a significant amount of good.

Ironically, when the same population was asked, "How do you view the nature of human beings?" over 80 percent indicated that they are both good and evil, and almost 15 percent shared the belief that humans are more good than they are evil. Less than 7 percent shared the belief that by nature, humans are more evil than good.

If one listens to the evening news in many major cities in the United States, however, or if the rate at which we incarcerate our citizens is considered, then there seems to be some confusion in terms of what is believed, what is practiced, and the behaviors that are usually displayed. Despite the knowledge that many good people do inhabit the earth, the perceived evil nature of human beings continues to be of concern in many cultures around the world.

Individuals who hold very strong positive beliefs about life, tend to give the impression that they possess many of the answers to life's enigmatic concerns. Furthermore, some individuals often find it incomprehensible that others cannot see things from their

Why Are You Here?

perspective, or they refuse to do so. It is almost as if some people are entitled to their strong beliefs, and they are entitled to share them, while others are not allowed to do likewise.

I have met individuals who will tell you for sure exactly what will happen to you when you die. In fact, in the January 2022 poll, most respondents (over 40 percent) indicated that what happens to you when you die depends on your religion. This implies that if they are right, the same type of segregation that we see here on earth along religious lines, should be expected to continue in the afterlife.

"Good" people, according to them, will supposedly end up in a place of happiness and peace, while "evil" ones will suffer eternal torment. Could they be right? Do they know something that others don't? I know some individuals who died, and, like many others, they led lives that were less than perfect, while they were here. Based on those beliefs, it makes me wonder not only where they finally ended up, but also whether some of them could be in the group in which I end up, when my time comes.

Over 35 percent of the January 2022 poll respondents feel that, in the end, one just ceases to exist. From an existential perspective, historically, this belief system has resulted in significant anxiety for many individuals, who have thought about the possibility of death being the end. What is certain, is that we humans like to exist. The idea, of even the remote possibility of non-existence, is enough to cause at least some to panic and to live their lives in fear.

I believe individuals are entitled to their own beliefs, especially when it pertains to matters like religion, how they should live their lives, and what they choose to embrace, where death is concerned. After all, who among us can say with some certainty that they know what happens when we die.

Over 95 percent of the members of my very large family are now deceased. Surely, I have far more experience with death, dying, and grieving than many people who I know. Yet, I cannot claim to know any more about what happens after death than anyone. Neither would I give the impression that my experiences are any more profound than those of others from small families, from those who have experienced only a single loss of a close family member or no losses as yet.

We do, however, know certain things from religious teachings about life that just make sense and on which

Why Are You Here?

many individuals, regardless of their religious persuasions, are inclined to agree. From my Buddhist studies, for example, the Five Reflections by the Buddha just make sense to me, and I am yet to find anyone who cares to disagree with them. These are the Five Reflections in Buddhism:

1. I will get older.
2. I will get sick.
3. I will die.
4. I will be separated from all that I care about.
5. I am responsible for my actions.

I am sure there are those who might be willing to debate the reflections. However, it is not an activity in which I would choose to engage. Many individuals, for example, spend a significant amount of their money on things that they think will help them maintain their youth. Still, to my knowledge, no one has discovered how to do that successfully yet. Please understand, I think if one wishes to slow the aging process, and there are many who wish to do so, they have the liberty to use whatever means they feel will help them accomplish that goal.

But it is how some people decide to go about the matter that I find particularly interesting. I know a man, for example, who is currently in his eighties. If you met him, many observations are immediately apparent. Firstly, he walks with a cane, which is not unusual at his age. Many people in their eighties need walking assistance. Secondly, he has wrinkled skin (common signs of aging also). This is not unusual either, because, as skin ages, it tends to wrinkle in places.

Interestingly, however, all the hairs on this man's head and on his face are jet black, even his eyebrows. He dyes them regularly, because he associates jet black hair with youthful look, and apparently, he is not ready to let go of that idea any time soon. I often wonder though whether the frequent use of hair dyes could be contributing to his aging in other ways. Still, it's his life, and he can choose to do as he sees fit.

"Why are we here?" The short answer, I believe, is that we can speculate all we want. We just do not know for sure. Even so, there are many ideas around, that seek to provide answers or at least reasonable explanations, and many individuals would willingly give an answer as well.

I believe embracing some type of belief system is better than not believing in anything at all. I also feel that because what we believe can have such a strong influence on how we behave and how we choose to live our lives, it is imperative that we think very seriously about ideas that we choose to embrace, or groups to which we decide to belong.

I am aware that some individuals may choose to conform to ideologies or groups, because of the sense of belonging that it provides them. That sense of belonging tends to help them avoid isolation and loneliness, which are sometimes very common in many segments of our society.

But I have also known individuals, who have been seriously traumatized by conforming to ideas that sounded innocent enough, or they may have even been presented to them with lofty promises of happiness and self-fulfillment in return for their membership. Those promises were not fulfilled.

So, as it pertains to the idea of why we are here, I feel that it is one of those questions to which we may never find answers. I also believe that when we think about this question very deeply, what we may really be asking is an even deeper one: "What is our purpose?" The easy answer to that one, is that we don't know for sure either. Various speculative ideas also abound about that question and from religious perspectives as well. Still, we truly do not know.

In the January 2022 poll that was mentioned earlier, when asked the question, "Do you know what your purpose is?" Over 70 percent responded in the affirmative. When those same individuals were asked, "If you were dying today, would you say that you fulfilled your life's purpose?" Over 50 percent said yes, while a close 45 percent said no.

Whether one is asked, "Why are you here?" or "Do you know what your purpose is?" It seems that it is something worth thinking about, and many individuals do spend a great deal of time trying to determine the reasons. How, however, can one really know for sure? Is it doing something at which one is exceptional? Is it the extent to which one enjoys a profession or a job? Is it doing something that is unique? Is it finding ways to have fun and enjoy life?

What I have learned is that we might really be in trouble when it comes to trying to answer questions like those. Let's face it, we don't know who we are, and we don't know why we are here. So, how are we supposed to live lives that could be considered meaningful? Perhaps it is no wonder there is so much chaos, evil, and suffering in the world. We are yet to know ourselves.

Yet, for many, the good news is that we are hopeful beings. Even though many individuals might not be able to say why they are here, when asked, "How does the future look to you?" 55 percent indicated that it looks very good.

Despite those views, however, it is noteworthy that over 40 percent of respondents view the future as "uncertain." How an uncertain view of the future could be affecting how some people choose to live their lives is certainly an area that begs for further exploration.

Like many other individuals, you may be trying to find your rightful place in the world. You are trying to find your purpose. Just what you are supposed to do here? In that regard, you are certainly not alone. What I have found is that although some people say that they know what their purpose is, deeper conversations with them reveal that they may have strong suspicions about the matter. However, like the rest of us, they really do not know.

There are those also, who feel that because they have certain "gifts" or "talents" in a particular activity, that is their purpose. Does that mean that if you excelled at car racing or at playing football, your sole purpose here was to engage in those activities? What about those who do not excel at anything, or those who have not identified any gifts or talents, does it imply that they have no purpose? And how about those who believe they are here solely to have fun and enjoy their lives? Does it mean that if you are not hedonistic by nature you have no purpose either?

Maybe everyone has a special purpose, but perhaps they have not been able to identify what it is. Just days before she died, I recall having a conversation with my paternal grandmother about whether she thought she had fulfilled her purpose here on earth, and what she thought her legacy was. Without thinking about it, she responded that her legacy was her nine children, all her grandchildren, and her great-grandchildren.

Now that I am older, I reflect on the conversation that I had with my grandmother, and it makes me wonder. Does that mean that my friends, and even some of my close relatives, who have no children, have no purpose or legacy, and those who have many children, have more legacy and more purpose?

We could continue this discussion about why we are here ad nauseam. We could also approach the question

Why Are You Here?

from diverse perspectives. Yet, I think we would still end up at the place where we began. It is one of those questions by which we have been intrigued for ages, and to which generations have consistently sought answers. Even so, we are no closer to uncovering the answer than any of our predecessors were.

Many individuals will still tell you that they know what their purpose is. They may say that their vocation is their calling. They may feel that what they are doing is so enjoyable that they could never imagine ever doing anything else. But is that one's purpose? Is that a person's reason for being? Perhaps, if they think so, and if they feel in their heart that it is so, then, for that individual, it could be as they think. Who can judge anyone for what they believe, or who can say otherwise?

After all, we know so very little about our lives. Therefore, apart from heart-felt feelings or gut feelings, what do we have to go by? How can we really know what our purpose is? What do we have to guide us? We can only trust our intuition and give whatever we feel we should be doing our very best. That decision could bring us some comfort. However, simply because we believe something or because it may bring us comfort, still does not mean that it is correct.

For many individuals, what they do brings them great satisfaction and rewards, while for others, there may be frustration and longing for something more enjoyable than what they are doing. Others spend years, a lifetime even, searching for that one thing that could bring peace of mind and satisfaction into their lives. Somehow, they always seem to come up short. That could be because they simply are not sure what to look for, or they may not have someone to guide them.

Several years ago, I asked a dying friend if he thought he had fulfilled his purpose here on earth. He thought about it in a very perplexing manner, before replying with a very emphatic, "Hell, no! I still haven't figured out what it is." I said to him, "Because you didn't figure out what it is, doesn't necessarily mean that you didn't find it or you didn't fulfill it. Maybe you fulfilled your purpose without realizing it, but you are just not aware of it." To which, he responded, "Could be."

I continued, "You are humble, you are kind, you are empathetic, and you helped many people in different ways, throughout your life. Maybe that was your purpose—to just be who you have been, but you didn't realize it. By being yourself, you have been a good example to others."

Why Are You Here?

"I suppose," he responded. "But I always thought it had to be something big, something more noticeable."

"You mean like walking on water or turning water into wine?" I asked. Then he laughed uncontrollably for a while, before saying, "To my recollection, only one man has ever done that, and I have not been anything like him." "Neither has anyone else, to my knowledge." I responded. "No one else has. Part of your purpose may also have been to be a good friend, like you have been to all of us, and you have been," I complemented him. "We learned a lot from you about friendship, and we appreciate you very much. Our lives would not have been the same without you." To that, he thought for a while longer before modestly replying, "That is a very kind thing for you to say. Thank you for saying that."

Perhaps something worth doing is for us to choose to coexist more harmoniously with our fellow human beings, to love and care for each other, and to engage in activities that will enable us to leave the world in a much better state than it was when we arrived. So many negative changes have taken place in the world, that despite major advances in many areas, the high prevalence of conditions such as depression and anxiety, serve as consistent reminders that significant changes are needed in others.

Important questions to ask therefore include: Even if my purpose has not been uncovered, can I still make a significant difference in the world? How would I know if I am making a difference, or if what I am doing matters? The easy answer is that sometimes it is not easy to tell whether what one does matters. By asking other questions, however, one may be able to gain some insight into whether they are engaged in activities that matter.

One could ask, for example, "Is my motive for engaging in this activity pure?" This could mean that the decision to engage in the activity was made purely to satisfy some greater good. Another question could be, "Apart from me, who else is going to benefit from the activity?" This is to ensure that the activity is not being done for selfish reasons. A third question could be, "After the activity is completed, will I and others feel good about what was done?"

That last question above may not apply to everyone. There are some individuals, for example, who could knowingly engage in activities to swindle others. Individuals, who engage in such activities, and some even make a living in that manner, may not be willing

Why Are You Here?

to ask that question. Nor will the answer really matter to them if they did. Notwithstanding, those are questions that many caring individuals could ask themselves to get an idea of whether what they are doing could be considered a noble deed.

We could also look at this issue from another perspective. If we considered the idea that we are here because we matter, then, it would be logical for us to conclude that whatever we do may also matter. Whether we recognize it or not, we must be making a difference in some way. If we could convince at least one other person to think likewise and to behave as if their existence and the activities in which they engage really does matter, we could most certainly conceptualize a world that is different from the one that we now inhabit.

Following are some ideas that could be considered, as one tries to figure out their purpose.

- In the grand scheme of things, although we might not be sure of what our purpose is, it is reasonable to assume that there is a good reason for all of us to be here. Whether we are geniuses or we are intellectually challenged, whether we have a profession that required several years of formal schooling, or we are engaged in activities that required very little or no formal schooling, we all have a reason to be here, and we each have important roles to play in the lives of others. Everyone could not be the CEO of a corporation. Someone must mop the floors, clean the toilets, and take out the garbage, and someone must oversee human resources and financial matters, because they are essential office functions. Think of what things would be like, if some services were discontinued even for a few days, or if they were absent altogether. Yet, they are functions that many workers tend to take for granted. They may not even recognize janitors and others as essential workers in their organizations. When they are considered as essential, however, and they are treated as such, a better sense of appreciation is apparent, for the role that each plays in the smooth running of the organization. If we look at our world as one huge organization in which everyone has an essential role, then, perhaps we might also develop a much better appreciation for the essential nature of everyone's existence, whether it is apparent to us or not. We might also get to appreciate the void that is left in families, and in society, when a member ceases to exist. Everyone has worth. Even if it is to give someone else a reason to feel empathy toward another person or to get them to perform a single act of kindness. It is still reason enough for someone to exist. Humans, however, like to look for big reasons. And by doing so, quite often we miss the smaller ones, which, in many cases, are just as significant as the grander ones.

- Even if you thought you didn't have reason to focus on yourself before, start developing the idea that you matter, and that you are an essential feature of the universe. Even if you find yourself in a state of poverty or in another situation that is very stressful, know that you still matter. If you were accustomed to viewing yourself as being on the lowest rung on the ladder, it is time for you to start realizing that every rung on the ladder has an essential role to play. If one rung is ever defective or if it is excluded, the ladder is compromised. It is just not able to function as efficiently. One's reason for being, also has no bearing on one's physical appearance, one's race or ethnicity, where one lives, how much formal education one received, or how much wealth one may have accumulated. Some of my friends in the rural area of Jamaica from which I originated can neither read nor write very well. They just never had the opportunity to be exposed to formal education for them to exploit their academic capabilities. Nor did they get the opportunity to travel overseas to see other parts of the world like I did. Yet, it is a delight for me to call them, visit them, when I am there, and spend time reasoning with them. Surely, they may not be able to use big words or flamboyant language, but what they say in their own simple terms makes just as much sense, and they are as much of a joy to be with as my colleagues, who possess many years of formal schooling. Over the years, I have noticed also, that some of those individuals do have many admirable, compensatory attributes. They are authentic, they are loyal and dependable, and I have learned many life lessons from them, based on their own life experiences. Owing to the very enriching qualities that they portray, I know for sure that they are in my life for very important reasons. I also know that it is because of my long and very positive association with them, that I now possess the skills and the gift of being able to relate to others on any level. Indeed, I know that it is because of their association that I am drawn to those in any society, who may be less advantaged, and why I feel so at home with them. There was a time when we lived similar lives.

- There was a time in my mid-teenage years, that I call the "searching period." At that time, some of my peers were experimenting with sex and substances and they were partying heavily. For various reasons however, I figured out, since I commenced studying human behavior, that my interests were primarily in matters that were of an existential nature. From then on, I was convinced that there must be a great deal more to life than what I was experiencing. Therefore, I embarked on a quest to "discover myself." I started studying various religions, metaphysics, spirituality, hermeneutics, the existence of secret societies, and other subjects that seemingly were not of interest to most of my peers. At that time, most of my close associations were with men in my father's age group. They took me under their wings, they gave me access to books that I didn't even know existed, and they educated me on the ways of the world. Those early exposures placed me in a position in which I was far ahead of my peers when it came to my grooming and my education in the school of life. It made me feel that I was called to be of greater service to humanity. The biggest lesson that I learned from very early was that despite my very humble beginnings, I was destined to make significant changes in the lives of others. When I look back now, I can honestly say that I have done so. To do so, however, meant that I had to recognize that my self-discovery was an essential part of my existence, but it is not an event. Rather, it is a lifelong process with daily challenges, and enormous ones too. Notwithstanding, there are many guides and there are guideposts along the way. One must know how to recognize them, and how to apply the lessons. Otherwise, it is quite easy to get stuck in one place or to lose one's way altogether. I know individuals who fall into both categories. There was a time in my life also, when

Why Are You Here?

I was determined to uncover possible reasons why some individuals, even some close relatives, were in my life. They brought so much hurt, stress, unhappiness, and pain. I was convinced that there must be other lessons for me as well. Then I started telling myself that they could be there for one of two reasons. Either to teach me love, patience, and tolerance—at which I failed miserably on many occasions—or to remind me of the type of person that I must never allow myself to become. Over the years, however, I have learned to be more accepting and less judgmental of others, because all human beings, including myself, have rough edges that could use some polishing. Therefore, I no longer waste precious time that I could use to help others, trying to figure out why some people are in my circle. Whether I understand it or not, I have learned to trust the universe enough to know that they are there for a reason. My responsibility is to understand that, and to accept them unconditionally. That does not imply that it is ever easy to do so. However, it is a necessary step if one is to live a fulfilling life. Despite that, however, whatever time I have left in this world is far too precious for me to spend on trying to figure out the "why." They are my fellow human beings. We happen to be from different circumstances, but we complement each other, sometimes-even in ways that I have come to realize I will never understand. Yet, our lives would never have been the same without each other. On the other hand, I also recognize that some of my biggest life stressors do come from some of my peers and from some of my closest family members. They are insincere, they are envious, competitive, and unsupportive, and if they get the chance, they will do or say things that are very hurtful. Therefore, I must know who they are, and how they operate. I must also be mindful that as stressful as it can be at times, I can never allow them to occupy front row seats in my life. While we are on the subject, let us not, even for one minute, naively pretend that the world is one large expanse of good and positivity. There is a great deal of goodness in this world. Sadly, however, there is a fair share of negativity and evil as well. Knowing to recognize that they both exist and knowing what to embrace and what to avoid, are essential aspects of everyone's existence.

- If you are doing something that you do not enjoy, understand that you always have other options. Throughout your life, you can excel at more than one thing. Therefore, confining yourself to doing just one thing, can be self-limiting, and it can result in unnecessary stress. First, examine the situation that you are in very deeply. Try to uncover the reason that you find your situation stressful. Perhaps, your passion lies in doing something else. Perhaps, you feel you are not earning as much, or maybe the problem is your attitude toward what you are doing, or toward your coworkers, or your overall attitude could use some overhaul. Self-analysis could lead you on your journey toward greater self-discovery, and you would be surprised how discovering certain negative traits about yourself (you are probably good at them, because of your lifelong practice), acknowledging them, and being willing to change them, could make your life more enjoyable. After conducting your self-examination, if you find that it is not you that need to change, then, find something to do that you think will be more meaningful or more joyful. But try not to waste time and other resources, while fooling yourself that you are looking for your true "calling." Many undergraduate college students do that. They change their majors several times, because they are in search of something that they think might be easier or more enjoyable. Finally, they realize that they have been in school for seven or nine years. They realize that they owe a great deal of money, or that they wasted their parents' hard-earned money, and they have not yet earned their first degree. They cannot drop out of school either, because the only experience they have at that point is attending school, and they have not done a good job of it either. They are unprepared for life in the real world. Many individuals make career changes, and it is not until later in their lives that some individuals find a vocation that they enjoy. My friend David (not his real name), for example, was an emergency room physician for many years before he decided to start taking black and white photographs, which he loved. He

Why Are You Here?

did enjoy practicing medicine, and he touched many lives throughout the years that he spent in the medical field. Even so, he got to a point where he thought a change of career was necessary. Today, he has his own photography studio in a big city. His work is admired by many, and some of his pieces are simply exquisite.

- Find ways to enjoy whatever you are doing now. Sometimes, finding enjoyment in one's job or in one's relationship can be difficult, which can make life even more complicated. This could be because a bad choice was made initially, because one was young and inexperienced at the time, or because enough research or consultation was not done. Many individuals make career decisions that are based primarily on financial rewards, without considering other aspects of their choices. Later in their lives, however, they realize that they get very little or no enjoyment out of what they do, or even from the money that they make. If you are doing something and it is difficult to experience happiness from it, don't just quit either. Wait until you find a reasonable replacement for the position in which you are currently employed, before choosing to leave for another, about which you may know very little. Bear in mind that there is no perfect job or perfect workplace. Occasionally, some individuals trade one imperfect position for one that appears more attractive, only to realize later when it is too late that they did not make a better choice after all. Sometimes also, one position may have imperfect aspects. However, you could look at it from other perspectives. Make sure you consider it in its entirety and be grateful for the positive features that it provides.

- Never give up on your self-discovery and your self-understanding, and never fool yourself into thinking that you know enough about who you are. Remember, it is not an event. It is a process, a lifelong process.
- We do not exist in a vacuum. Consider how your choices and your decisions could affect others.
- When challenges arise, figure out what you need to do to bring about peace and speedy resolution. Still, never forget that very often they come at a very high price—a high price that is probably still worth paying.

Why Are You Here?

- There is enough hatred and unkindness in the world. Consistently look for opportunities to express love and kindness.
- Even with the billions of people in the world, there is a great deal of loneliness and isolation. Never miss the opportunity to befriend someone and to show that you care.
- Never do something for anyone and expect repayment in any form. It is your duty as a fellow human being to share with others. The universe is compensating you already. Sometimes, the satisfaction that is available from serving others may be all that you get. Learn to be content with that. You must recognize that it is still a great deal, especially if you know how to humbly embrace it.
- You will not always be happy. When you are down, however, it is important for you to understand that being down is also an integral part of the cycle of life. Learn to get back on your feet quickly, just like you did many times before.
- When you see someone down, extend a helping hand. Also provide whatever other assistance they may need to get back on their feet.

- Never forget those who helped you to get back on your feet when you were down. You may never get the opportunity to thank them personally but helping others in similar situations as you have been, is an excellent way of expressing gratitude.
- Constantly, look for opportunities to serve others. Giving of yourself, especially of your time, is one of the greatest gifts that anyone could give.
- Learn to listen. Listen to yourself and to others. Everyone has something to say—something that is worth a listening ear.
- Never get the idea that you are superior to anyone. You are not. Another individual's circumstances may be different from yours, or they may have less access or opportunities to resources than you do, but greater access and more opportunities do not make you superior to anyone.
- Learn to meditate. The reason many individuals cannot find peace is because they haven't realized yet that it is not external. It is deep within all of us. Learn to access it.
- Every single day, do something to make someone's day much better. Sometimes, it takes just a

kind word or even a smile. It does not have to be something big. A small gift is still a gift.
- Learn to share. Consider how much you brought with you when you came into the world, and, regardless of how much you amass during your time here, consider how much you will take with you when you leave. Share what you have gathered with those who may not have perfected the art of gathering as much as you did.
- Pick your battles. Sometimes it is good to get involved, but at other times, it may be best if you know how to mind your own business.
- Know that your point-of-view may not always be the only one. It may not be the right one either.
- Because you think it, doesn't mean that you must express it. There are times to speak up and times to keep quiet. You learn more from listening than you do from talking.
- Understand that other people's property is just as valuable as yours. Learn to respect other people's possessions. If you are a multi-millionaire living in a mansion, the poor man who lives in a one-bedroom shack still values it as his home. It is just as valuable to him as yours is to you.

- Learn to respect others. Each person's circumstance may be different, but we all have at least one thing in common. We are all human beings.
- Recognize the good attributes that you possess but recognize also that others may have what you don't. It is important for us to learn to share.
- Learn to embrace some experiences that you may have viewed negatively. Some of life's most powerful lessons come from being in the strangest situations and from things that occur at the most inopportune times.
- Find value in other people and respect what they do as much as you value and respect yourself and what you do. You may be one of the best cardiac surgeons. However, you may not be able to manicure your own lawn as well as your landscaper does, or you may not be able to diagnose what is wrong when your car malfunctions. You may not even know how to change your own flat tire. Surely, your time is valuable, and you can pay to get those things done. Still, it is important to recognize those who help to make your life easier. I recall an incident that occurred at the home of one of my past supervisors. We were at

his home, and his driver asked his maid for water to drink. After he drank the water, my supervisor scolded the maid for giving him the water in one of the "good" glasses that was reserved for special guests, rather than giving it to him in a plastic cup. Years later, when my supervisor was very ill, it was that driver who took him to his doctor visits and picked up his medicines for him. Although I said nothing then, I got a lesson from it, and I still remember it today.

- Take care of yourself.
- Love yourself but learn to love others. Love is the best antidote for hatred in the world.
- Be kind to yourself but be kind to others.
- You could live your entire life and not uncover your purpose. Still, recognize that just because you don't figure out something, doesn't make it any less important.
- Cover your bases. Do what is good. Do what is right. What do you have to lose?

3

The Role of Parents

THE PROCESS OF reproduction, especially human reproduction, is one of the most complex, yet one of the most interesting phenomena in the entire world. It is how new life is consistently introduced. It ensures the continuity of our existence, and the existence of other species. Our reproductive capability is an integral part of the Grand Design.

Just think about it for a moment, as we explore basic Biology—Biology 101. Except for those very rare cases in which hermaphrodites are known to reproduce, everyone is the product of a male and a female. The female gender being the one that is designed for offspring bearing. In the human species, the design and the process of reproduction are undoubtedly both beautiful and enjoyable.

Human females are born with all the eggs that they will have throughout their lives, and they store them in their ovaries. Males, on the other hand, produce new sperms every day. They take weeks to mature and they store them in their epididymis until they are ready to be released. Even before female minds and bodies are developed enough for reproduction, somewhere just before the teenage years, they start releasing eggs from their ovaries.

Correspondingly, a little later than females, but just before their teenage years, males usually start producing sperm cells. They release them either by self-stimulation (masturbation), sexual intercourse, or through a natural process termed wet dreaming or nocturnal emission. If the time is right and sexual activity occurs between a male and female, although millions of sperm are released when a male ejaculates, a single sperm cell penetrates a single egg that was released from an ovary of the female, and fertilization takes place, usually inside the fallopian tubes of the female's body.

Development of the fetus inside the female is continuous, until around nine months or so, when a new human being is introduced into the world. The two people that are involved in this activity, the producers of the egg and sperm, are called the biological parents of the new human.

Nowadays, with advances in the reproductive sciences, there are variations of the scenario just described. For example, a woman's ovaries can be stimulated to release many eggs. The eggs can be harvested and fertilized outside of her body and the developing embryos could either be implanted inside her uterus, inside the uterus of another female, or they could be kept frozen for implantation later. In either case, a sperm from the man and an egg from the woman are the basic building blocks of every human being. The parents are the ones who are usually charged with the responsibility of nurturing, caring, and molding their offspring into a fully functioning, well-adjusted, productive human being.

The role of parents in the lives of children has been undergoing significant changes over the years. Still, there is the expectation that despite significant changes in many areas, as scientific knowledge continues to advance, many aspects of the conventional method of producing new humans will remain intact. Regardless of the angle from which it is viewed, the process of successfully producing, guiding, and helping a human being to develop from the womb to the tomb, is one of life's most difficult, yet most rewarding undertakings.

What responsibilities do parents have for their children? What are they expected to contribute to their lives, and for how long? Human reproduction and the parenting that goes along with it, have become very hot topics in recent years. They are broad matters, and they involve numerous controversial aspects as well. It is not possible to adequately address those matters, for example, without mentioning words like reproductive rights, pro-life and pro-choice, abortion, adoption, gender-related identity, abuse, abandonment, neglect, divorce, parental alienation, paternity fraud, rape, incest, and several other very important concerns.

Many of those concerns are at the forefront of today's parenting culture, and they have a marked influence on the lives of parents and children, and on society. Many therapists who work with parents, can attest to how emotionally charged conversations can get, when they work with some families, who present with challenges stemming from some of those concerns.

Still, it is not within the scope of this very small volume to explore those matters further. One thing that must be stressed, however, is that many family situations do affect the lives of individuals negatively. Many individuals also feel very strongly that parents have a moral responsibility to care for their children, to provide for them, protect them, raise them well, and ensure that they develop and mature into their best selves.

The Role of Parents

Basically, whatever parents and society do or do not do, will affect the lives of their children and the adults that they eventually become. Loving, healthy, well-adjusted, happy parents are expected to raise children who exhibit those same qualities. On the other hand, having children is not like baking a cake. If the ingredients of a cake are measured in the right proportions and they are mixed homogeneously and baked for the desired amount of time, there is a very good chance that the end-product will be as exquisite as it was expected.

Cakes are inanimate, however. They do not have genetic components. Neither do they have emotions and many characteristics that are ascribed to human beings. If a baker made a mistake and their product was not as attractive or as palatable as it was expected, they could always mix a fresh batch of ingredients and try again.

Some mistakes that parents make, even before a child is born, could spell serious trouble for the child, for the family, and for society, sometimes even for generations. If a woman uses certain drugs (prescribed or unprescribed) or alcohol during her pregnancy, she runs the risk of giving birth to a child that could be born with developmental and behavioral challenges that could affect them for their entire life.

And it is not just what happens in mothers' bodies that could have adverse effects on their offspring. There are genetic conditions that parents carry (knowingly or not), behavioral decisions that they or grandparents made, or home and other environmental concerns that can have negative effects on the lives of their children, and they could even continue to affect them as adults.

A child that was raised in an environment in which fighting, domestic violence, and abuse were prevalent, for example, is very often not expected to be as well-adjusted or as happy as one that was raised under more positive circumstances. Children, whose lives were favorable for their successful advancement at every stage of their development, have a far better chance of having a promise-filled life. The very negative behaviors that are often exhibited by many adults in our society, can be traced to how their parents interacted with each other and with them, and to the environments in which they were raised.

Throughout children's lives, there are many interactions between their parents that can affect them and who they become as adults. Take the situation involving marriage and divorce. Marital situations involving a loving mother and father who live together with their children in the same home is usually regarded as the best situation in which to raise children. Even so, close to a half of all first marriages in America today end in divorce, within the first eight to ten years.

Married individuals took vows that they would remain with each other forever. At the inception of their relationship, they cared for each other very deeply, and they intended for their union to last. They did not just wake up one morning and decided to part ways either. Usually, their relationships start to break down a long time before they get to the divorce court, and their children had been affected negatively from much earlier as well.

As if the relationship between parents was not bad enough, the entire process and the duration of a divorce is often much worse for children. For a very long time, many children carry the scars that they developed from seeing their parents interacting negatively with each other. It should not be too surprising, therefore, that many children whose parents divorced are also more likely to divorce as well.

Many other situations that involve parents, have negative effects on children throughout their lives and even on successive generations. It is paramount, therefore, for individuals, who are from backgrounds that may not have been very enriching, to engage in their own self-discovery and self-understanding very early in their lives. Hopefully, even before they decide to marry and to have children.

Of course, we know that many children are introduced into a world in which the odds are already stacked heavily against them. They may have been the products of unplanned pregnancies, which placed them in disadvantageous positions from the outset. And even if they were from homes with two-parent families, we know how difficult some relationships can be, and how they sometimes have the tendency to get worse, following the advent of children.

Beginning with pre-marital counseling, the importance of professional intervention in many relationships, cannot be overemphasized. Still, we also know that although many individuals have been aware that they could use some help with addressing challenges from their childhood, they never seek the help that they need.

Consequently, they enter relationships with other individuals, who also have their own challenges. They get caught up in their feelings of lust and infatuation, and they lose focus on their self-development. Those feelings

The Role of Parents

drive the behaviors of many individuals in our over-romanticized society. They are simply recipes for disaster both for the adults themselves and for the children that result from their interactions.

In America today, it has become very trendy to raise children in single-parent households. I would like to make it very clear from the outset, that I am very aware of the situation regarding many mothers who bear the burden of raising children alone, either because they were conceived with irresponsible fathers, because the fathers died, or for many other undesirable or unfortunate reasons. Those are not the situations to which I am referring.

My reference is to other factors that lead to the exclusion of fathers from families or from their children's lives altogether. Some mothers, for example, wish to experience motherhood, but they do not want men to be involved in their lives or in the lives of their children. They may wish to be mothers, but they have no desire to be wives. As popular as that decision may be nowadays, very often it has devastating consequences for children who are raised without the involvement of their fathers.

Still, although there are some families in which fathers have been absent for many generations, the issue of raising children in single-mother households is a very emotionally charged subject. From a historical perspective, especially in minority communities, some mothers were encouraged to exclude fathers from their children's lives. They even received many of the resources from the government that fathers would have been expected to provide. What was not taken into consideration, however, were the emotional and other essential contributions that fathers bring to the parenting table, and the damage that is inflicted when they are absent.

Even in the New Millennium, controversies surrounding whether fathers are important in families remain very strong. This is despite an overabundance of convincing evidence, which point to the fact that there has been a fatherhood crisis in America for decades.

Additionally, especially since the advent of "no-fault divorces" in the seventies, efforts to get many Americans to remain in their marriages long-term, have not been very successful. We now know that in numerous cases in which fathers are absent from children's lives, or when they are not actively involved in their upbringing, the children often suffer.

Research findings consistently affirm that fathers bring very positive and lasting benefits to the lives of

The Role of Parents

children. Yet, there are still forces within our society that are promoting ideas to the contrary. The absence of fathers from children's lives has been linked to many of the social problems that are encountered in our society today. The findings can be quite disturbing. According to the United States Census Bureau and other notable agencies, children that are raised without fathers are at a greater disadvantage in many areas of their lives than their peers, who are raised in intact two-parent households.

- Over 24 million children in America are raised in homes without fathers (historically, America is the country in the world with the most homes with absent fathers).
- They are four times more likely to be poor.
- They are two times more likely to be obese.
- They are more likely to commit crimes and become incarcerated.
- They are more likely to use drugs and alcohol.
- They are more likely to be abused and neglected.
- Girls are seven times more likely to be pregnant in their teenage years.

- Children who are raised without fathers are more likely to be depressed (depressed individuals are more likely to kill themselves).
- Children who are raised without fathers have more academic and behavioral challenges.

Another major concern involves messages that children receive from being raised in some single-parent households, especially if the mother is unsupportive of the father being involved in their lives. The concern is two-fold. Both boys and girls may get the message that fathers are not important. Many girls grow up and repeat the father-absent cycle with their children.

The other concern pertains to negative messages that boys receive, when they are raised in those situations. When boys receive consistent negative messages, especially from their mothers, which suggest that fathers are not important, they could act out those roles in their families when they become fathers. After all, if they were raised with the idea that mothers alone can raise children successfully, what incentive should they have to remain involved in the lives of children that they fathered? Why would they want to contribute positively to their children's development?

The Role of Parents

The point of this chapter is to show how the roles that parents play in children's lives could influence their development and affect their lives in various ways. The circumstances under which an individual was raised can, and it often does, have an influence on their life. Even so, there comes a time when adults must learn to stop blaming their parents for the things that they did. They must be willing to stop focusing on past negative events and take responsibility for their own lives.

Many adults usually develop the understanding that parents are not infallible, and they sometimes do things that are not in their children's best interest. They must also recognize that parents may have realized some of their parenting skills were questionable.

Parents usually endeavor to raise their children with love and care. Unfortunately, quite often, it is not until children become parents themselves that they begin to realize how challenging raising children really is. Sadly, by then, many parents are already deceased.

Even with the enormous role that parents play in guiding children, they are not the only ones, whose influence is paramount. Indeed, grandparents, other extended family members, peers, religious and social groups, teachers, and the wider society play very important roles as well.

The unquestionably positive roles played by my parents, my grandparents, my siblings, and other close family members and friends in my life, cannot be overstated. Even so, very rarely do I get the opportunity to acknowledge or to express gratitude for the individuals, who have had exceptional influences on my life and for the person who I have become.

When I was ten-and-a-half to eleven-years-old and attending elementary school in Jamaica, my classroom teacher was a very tall, white, cigar-smoking, American Peace Corps volunteer by the name of Mr. Mark Wilson (not his real name). At that age, I had never been around white people before. In fact, Mr. Wilson was the first white person I had come to know, and I used to wonder how he ended up in a place like rural Jamaica, where I was raised.

Looking back now, he must have been a very special person from the inception for deciding to join the Peace Corps voluntarily, and reside away from family and friends in the rural area of a third world country. He was an excellent teacher. He cared about his students, and he was heavily invested in ensuring that they were learning.

The Role of Parents

At that time, only one university was in Jamaica. From high schools across the island, students who showed academic promise, were funneled into the university to study various disciplines. However, to enter those high schools, students must have been successful in what was termed the Common Entrance Examination, which they took somewhere around age eleven.

Students, who were unsuccessful in the Common Entrance Examination, or those who did not take the test, spent a few more years to complete elementary school. They went to one of the few technical or vocational high schools, or they sought entry-level jobs. At every level of the education system, students were being excluded.

One morning, just before lunchtime, Mr. Wilson summoned me to his desk. "Percy," he said. Are you ready to take the upcoming Common Entrance Examination?" "No sir," I replied. "I have not been preparing for it." "What!" he said. "Why not?" "Because" I said. "As soon as school is dismissed, I have to head home to take care of the animals."

My father was not considered wealthy by any means. Still, he owned several properties at various locations, and he had several cows and dozens of goats that my brothers and I cared for daily, before and after school.

Fulfilled

We milked the nannies each morning and sometimes we slaughtered the billys for their meat. It is one of the reasons that I have been a vegetarian. It wasn't easy caring for an animal and then killing it for its meat.

"Come with me when the lunch bell rings," Mr. Wilson said. All kinds of questions went through my mind. "Go with him?" I wondered. "Where could we possibly be going? I will be missing my lunch." Anyway, when the lunch bell rang, I thought about making a run for it. However, I came to my senses very quickly, because I knew I would have to return to his class after having my lunch, and I would have had no way of explaining what I did, without telling him a lie.

"We are going to see the principal," he said. "What did I do?" I asked. "You didn't do anything," he said. "I am going to ask him to put your name on the list to take the Common Entrance Examination in a few weeks, I know you are ready, and you will do very well in high school." Shocked was the only word that came to my mind.

My people were farmers. No one in my immediate family on either side had ever been to high school as far as I knew. I didn't even know what high school really was. Plus, that was what he thought. What would my father think? He was the only one who could decide.

"Wait here," he said, when we arrived at the principal's office. I stood outside the door as my teacher went inside. I had never listened so intently to any conversation in my life. Over fifty years later, I can still repeat every single word that was uttered. "Teacher," he said to the principal. "This boy that I have here with me, I would like you to add him to the list of students that you are sending for the Common Entrance Examination." "Where is he?" The principal asked. "Whose boy is he?" "Percy," Mr. Wilson called. "Yes sir," I responded. "Come in here."

Then, hungrily (because I was missing my lunch, and my stomach was accustomed to having it at that time daily) and anxiously, I entered the principal's office. I was a student at the school for six years already, and I had never spoken to him before. Neither did I have any reason to visit his office. "This is my student Percival Ricketts," Mr. Wilson said. To my surprise, the principal knew who my father was. "Are you Walter Ricketts's son?" He asked. "Yes sir," I said. Then, as if I was invisible or of no significance, he turned to Mr. Wilson and said, "Oh, I know the family. They are not college material. They have land and animals, and they work on their farm. I am not adding his name to the list. I send children who I know will pass and I send my friend's children. I am not sending him." "Thank you," Mr. Wilson said, and we went back to the classroom. "Don't worry," he said. "Don't listen to a word that he just said. Not only are you college material, you are going to do very well. Come to me after school. We will find a way. I am walking home with you this evening to speak with your father. You can go get your lunch now." "Ok, sir," I said.

With the tears still streaming down my face, instead of going to lunch, I went to find my older brother to appraise him of what had transpired. At that time, my older brother was always very serious, and he protected me with all his being. After all, we had lost our older sister and our younger brother a few years before, and that made us grow even closer. We were grieving together. My brother put his hand on my shoulder. He walked with me to have my lunch and he was able to console me successfully.

That must have been the longest afternoon that I had ever spent at that school. It seemed like the final bell would never ring. Finally, when the time came, and it rang, I went to see Mr. Wilson as he had suggested, and we started the two-mile-or-so walk to my home. That evening, the walk seemed the longest it had ever been.

The Role of Parents

All the inquisitive children from my neighborhood walked closely beside us, and behind us. They were anxious to know why Mr. Wilson was walking with me, where he was going, and, of course, what we were talking about. I smiled, as I observed them attempting to listen keenly to what we were talking about, but they still didn't have a clue.

Looking back now; I am pretty sure Mr. Wilson realized what was happening, because he did such a great job of distracting the other kids and making me feel at ease. We talked mainly about things that we passed along the way, my thoughts about life in the district where I lived, my family, the animals on my farm, and what I thought I wanted to do when I was older.

When we got to my home, my father was sitting under the big Ackee tree that was in our yard. That tree was much older than I was. As a mischievous young boy, I enjoyed climbing the Ackee tree to pick open fruits, although, at times I would go to the top as a hideout, to escape from doing chores. My father was listening to the radio while he was making bamboo fishing pots. I have never met anyone who made the types of fishing pots that he did. I remember one year, he entered two of his pots in the creative arts competition at the National

Denbigh Agricultural Show that was held every August around Independence time. His two pots won first and second place respectively.

It was such a long time ago. I cannot remember what my father was listening to on the radio that evening. In any case, I remember that as we got close to him, he got up, smiled, looked Mr. Wilson in his eyes, extended his right hand, and they greeted each other.

"What did my boy do?" he asked Mr. Wilson. "Nothing," my teacher responded. "You have a great kid here, Mr. Ricketts. He is one of the best kids in my class. That's why I am here. Percy is going to go places, but you must transfer him to another school. If he remains at the current school, he will never meet his full potential. So, you will have to start sending him to school in May Pen immediately."

I will never forget the look in my father's eyes. Over the years, I wondered what it must have been like to hear those words, not just from my teacher, but also from a White man from America. My father and Mr. Wilson chatted for a long time. I went to pick navel oranges for him in the backyard. My father also picked jelly coconuts for him. He drank the water from two of them, but he never ate the jelly inside.

The Role of Parents

Mr. Wilson gave one of the biggest burps I had ever heard, and we all laughed until I fell to the ground. It seemed like he was there talking to my father for hours. It must have been a very pleasant conversation for both of them, because they seemed very happy.

Later that evening, I told my father what had transpired at school earlier that day. I could sense his mixed emotions. What happened when we went to the principal's office made him angry, but at the same time, it was obvious that he still enjoyed Mr. Wilson's visit. Ironically, if the situation that occurred earlier did not take place, there would have been no reason for Mr. Wilson to have visited. There was a good chance that they may not have met each other either. When I was young, only on very rare occasions would parents ever visit their child's school or would they ever get an opportunity to meet their child's teacher.

That night, my father told me that he was going to take my teacher's advice and enroll me in the May Pen Primary school. This meant that I would have to get up very early, and I would have to take the bus to and from school every day. I was anxious about the unknowns, but I was also excited about the possibilities. I was very excited indeed.

Mr. Wilson had written a letter to the principal of the May Pen Primary school, and I picked it up from him at school the following day. In those days, most documents were handwritten. There were only a few typewriters, and there were no computers, certainly, not where I lived.

When I picked up the letter from Mr. Wilson, it was sealed. He addressed it, "The Principal, May Pen Primary School." Neither my father nor I knew what the contents were. Still, I was pretty sure there wasn't anything negative.

The following Monday morning at about 5:30 AM, my father woke me. We had some tea, and then we took the quarter-mile walk to wait for the bus to go to May Pen. This must have been only my third or fourth trip to the capital of our parish. I was looking forward to the trip.

The bus was very crowded. We both had to stand for the ten-mile journey into the town. I wore my shoes and my socks. Those days, the only time I wore my shoes was to Sunday school. At the May Pen Primary school, all the children wore shoes and socks every day. This meant that I would be doing likewise.

We arrived at the school very early, and we waited outside the principal's office for him to arrive. In my heart I knew that my experience with this principal was going to be much different from what happened with the last

The Role of Parents

one just days before. Looking around the buildings and seeing the children from the big town didn't bring me much comfort though. I was glad my dad was with me. I was tall for my age, and I was very slim. I was a very quiet country boy and I felt like a fish out of water already.

My feet were killing me. I wasn't accustomed to wearing my shoes for that long, and it seemed my feet had grown another size since I had put them on early that morning. "If I make it," I thought. "If I get into this school, I will have to get up very early every morning, rain or shine, to catch the bus. And I will have to travel alone. My father will never be traveling with me again. Plus, I will miss going to school at Rock River Primary. My brothers, and all my friends would still be going there, and I didn't know anyone at the new school yet either."

The principal, Mr. Smith (not his real name), was very tall. He looked like he was about my father's age. He wore strange-looking glasses with thick lenses, and he had on a long-sleeved white shirt with an odd-looking bowtie. His khaki pants were very baggy, and he moved very hurriedly. His speech was very quick, and he was noticeably very polite.

"Good morning," he said very assertively, as he shook my father's hand. Unbelievably, he did the same to me. I don't believe anyone had ever shaken my hand before that. His handshake was very firm. I thought he must have forgotten that I was a kid. With a handshake like that, he could have easily broken my hand.

We all smiled, as he led the way into his office. "What brings you gentlemen here today?" He enquired. "My name is Walter Ricketts, sir, and this is my son, Percival. We are from Rock River. His teacher, Mr. Wilson, gave me a letter to give to you, because he thinks my son will be much better off at this school." "Oh?" he remarked. "Let me see." My father handed him the letter, and he looked at it. Then he said, "Interesting. come with me." He continued, "Follow me." We went into an empty classroom, and he said, "Wait here."

About ten minutes later, Mr. Smith returned with three sheets of paper. One had some math problems, the other had sentences to be corrected, and the third was a blank sheet for answers. He also gave me a recently sharpened, new, Number 2 pencil.

They were problems that I had completed from my lower classes, at my now soon-to-be alma mater. They included long division, fractions, and percentages for the math, and grammar and parts of speech corrections for the English. I thought they were very simple, all of them.

The Role of Parents

I sat in the room with my father, and I completed the problems very quickly. He returned in about fifteen to twenty minutes to see how I was doing, and I told him that I was finished already. He looked them over, smiled, and then he said to my father, "Did you help him?" "No," my father said very assertively. "My son has always done well in school. That's why we are here."

"Okay, you come with me," he said. He brought me to another room by myself and he gave me other problems that were more advanced, but they also looked very familiar to me. This time, he asked his secretary to stay with me in that room. She was tall and slim. She was wearing high heels, a very tight-fitting red dress, and light red lipstick. She was beautiful, and she smelled sweet like roses.

When I was finished, I told the secretary. She told me to remain there while she took the papers to Mr. Smith. Soon, he came to the room. "I am very impressed," he said to me. "You did very well. Welcome to May Pen Primary School. I am going to place you with my A1 students in Class 6A. School starts tomorrow at 8:00 AM."

He shook my father's hand again then he shook mine. We thanked Mr. Smith, and we left the campus to have brunch in a little shop nearby. We were not accustomed to eating food from cafes and other eateries. In fact, we didn't have those types of establishments in my little district in the country. We had everything that we needed to eat at home. We grew what we ate, and we ate what we grew. We always prepared fresh food for ourselves every day.

I was very excited, and I could tell my father was bursting with pride also. The very next day, I started classes at my new school. Getting to school on the bus in the mornings was the most challenging part of my experiences at my new school. Still, I fitted in very quickly, I made many new friends, and they made me feel welcome. They enjoyed my stories about what it was like growing up in the country, but I did not care for life in the town at all.

Now that I am older, when I reflect on my life, I realize how lucky I was, and how some misfortunes can result in great opportunities. Although I no longer saw them every day, I still had my old friends at the other primary school, and then I got the opportunity to make new friends as well. Over fifty years later; individuals from both schools are still some of my best friends.

In January of 1968, I passed the Common Entrance Examination to attend the very prestigious Glenmuir

The Role of Parents

High School in May Pen. It was the formal start of my academic life. Space is too limited in this small volume to delve further in my life as a student at Glenmuir High School. Even so, the five years that I spent there fall among some of the most important times of my entire life.

If I may say so myself, with associate's, bachelor's, master's, and doctoral degrees, I think I have done quite well academically—not bad at all, for a quiet country boy, who was not viewed as "college material." Surely, it has been the result of hard work and determination. But none of it would have been possible without the support of many individuals, some of whom I feel obligated to mention.

Those individuals include my parents and grandparents, my older brother, Cleveland, some members of my extended family, and some members of a few other families, who provided me with love and support. Much of the credit for my success goes to the Peace Corps Volunteer, Mr. Mark Wilson. He saw something in me, and he believed in me, at a time when I did not even understand what that meant. Since migrating to the United States in 1990, I tried to locate Mr. Wilson to inform him of the very positive effect that he had on my life.

I did not know it at the time, but he was Jewish. I was able to locate him in Israel, where he was residing, and it was a very emotional moment for both of us. Still, even before I was able to contact him, every opportunity that I got to help someone, I usually thought of how he and others helped me, when I was younger. Mr. Wilson will always remain one of the greatest influences on my life, and he will always be one of my biggest heroes.

This has been one of my stories that demonstrated the influence that one teacher had on my life, and how parents and teachers can influence children's lives very positively. I am sure similar stories exist with numerous other individuals. Important as they are, however, quite often they go untold.

Additionally, there is a noticeable trend in our society today, in which some individuals give the impression that they are self-made. Consequently, they fail to express gratitude to those who helped them. It is important for us to reflect on our lives periodically, and to acknowledge those who helped us become who we are. Indeed, even if we were raised under disadvantageous circumstances, we just could not have gotten to our current destination without the help of others, even one person, who offered some assistance and provided some guidance at some point.

It is also very important for parents and other caregivers to remain mindful of the enormous responsibilities with which they are entrusted when children are in their care. Children look to parents and other adults for guidance and protection. Therefore, whatever adults do or say, can have significant influences on their lives. Adults simply cannot expect children to thrive, if they do not consistently provide them with the ingredients that they need to excel.

Reflecting on the following points could help individuals look at the roles that their parents and others played in their lives:

- The opportunity to parent is one of the most rewarding experiences that many individuals have throughout their lives. Even so, raising children, nurturing them, providing for their needs, and guiding them through the various stages of their development from birth until they become mature adults, can be rather challenging and stressful. What do you think your parents

would say, have been the most stressful parts of their lives?
- What would you say were the most challenging parts of your life as a child?
- How would you describe your relationship with your parents when you were growing up?
- How would you describe your relationship with your parents today?
- What would you say has been the most important lesson that you learned from your mom?
- What was the biggest lesson that you learned from your dad?
- What are some activities that your parents did with you that you have done, or you will do with your children?
- What are some activities that you will not be doing with your children?
- In many cases, parents do their best with raising their children. Would you agree?
- Would you say that your parents did a great job raising you? What do you wish they had done better?

The Role of Parents

- Have you ever expressed gratitude to your parents for raising you? If not, why not? When would be a good time to do so?
- Considering how well many individuals developed based on the love, guidance, and support that they received from their parents, what, if any obligations, do you think a person should have to his/her parents?
- Every family is different. When you assess your situation, what is your conclusion about the job that your parents did with raising you?
- Parents are not perfect. Sometimes they make mistakes. Still, rather than criticize them and point out areas where they could have done better, perhaps it would be more helpful for children to focus on areas in which parents excelled. Do you agree? List some positive things that your parents did for you.
- List some things that your parents did that you now think were negative.
- Rather than confronting your parents for things that they did that you think affected you negatively, would you consider consulting with a therapist to work through them?

Fulfilled

- A few years ago, I witnessed a friend crying. During a disagreement with her teenage daughter, the daughter said the following to her. "I didn't ask to come into this world. You were the one who decided that you wanted to have children. You brought me here. In case you haven't noticed, you are getting older. Who is going to take care of you when you can't help yourself anymore? I have my life to live. I am not planning to help you. Taking care of you is not my responsibility. You are responsible for yourself and for me. If you make good preparations, and you save enough money, I may do you the favor of choosing a nice nursing home for you, but I cannot promise you that I will visit." During the ensuing years, their relationship deteriorated significantly. The mother did make other arrangements for herself, and her daughter went to live with friends. What do you think about what the daughter said to her mother? If you were the daughter, is that something that you would have said to your mother? If you were the mother, what would you have done?
- In many areas of the world, families tend to be patrifocal. In America, however, many view

The Role of Parents

families as matrifocal. How was the family in which you were raised? Was it patrifocal, matrifocal, egalitarian, or single parented? Granted, you may have never been exposed to any other type of family than the one in which you were raised. Think about how your life today was shaped by the family in which you were raised.
- America has the most families in the world that are without fathers. Was there a father present in your home when you were growing up? If your answer is no, do you know why your father was absent?
- If your father was absent from your home when you were growing up, did you still have a relationship with him?
- If your father was present in the home when you were growing up, did you have a relationship with him?
- How has your relationship with your father, absent or present, affected your life as an adult?
- If you have children, would you say that your relationship with your children is much better than the relationship that you have with your parent of the same gender as you?

- What did your mother tell you about your father that encouraged you to have, or discouraged you from having a relationship with him?
- Write letters to both parents regarding how you feel about how they raised you. If the contents are positive, you may choose a convenient time to present the letters, or, you could mail them as a surprise. That could also be an excellent Mother's Day or Father's Day gift.
- If the letters that you write to your parents are negative, consider sharing them with a therapist, before presenting them to your parents. Sharing negative feelings about how you think you were raised may not be a great idea. However, some professional guidance and modifications could be beneficial.
- What about individuals other than your parents, who had a marked influence on your life? Do you remember them and the positive influences that they had? Have you expressed gratitude to them? Is that something that you think might be important for you to do? What do you think would be the best way for you to do so?

The Role of Parents

- Many parents play "games" when they are raising children. Not only are games hurtful to children, but also, they convey negative messages that have the potential to affect children throughout their lives. Some common games that parents are known to play include the following:
  - Having a favorite child that is treated differently from the other siblings.
  - Parentifying (treating the child as the other adult and using them to meet adult needs).
  - Alienating the children's affection from the other parent (deliberately engaging in inappropriate behaviors with the children or telling negative things about the other parent, that prevent them from desiring to have a close relationship with that other parent).
  - Displaying emotionally incestuous or covert incestuous behaviors (rather than sharing with another adult, using a child to meet emotional needs).
  - Using a child to spy on their other parent.
  - Doing things that give children the impression that one parent is better, cooler, or more loving than the other.

- Treating the child as a friend. This affects discipline because we do not discipline our friends.
- Refusing to keep the other parent in the loop when it comes to the child's welfare.
- Telling a child lies about the other parent. Some children spend their entire lives without knowing the truth about their other parent and it affects their relationship with them.
- Suggesting to a child that relatives on one side of a family are better than those on the other side, and discouraging the child from having a relationship with them.
- Calling the other parent names or speaking negatively about them in the presence of the child.
- Picking fights with the other parent or disrespecting the other parent while the child is present.
- Secretly recording conversations between parents and playing the recordings to a child to prove a point. In many cases, the parent doing the recording will not say what their involvement was before the recording started.

The Role of Parents

> So, the children only got one side of the story, which is usually negative. This is designed to make the other parent look bad.
> - Blaming the other parent for negative things that happen in the family, while taking credit for all the positive ones.

Can you think of "games" that your mom or dad played while you were growing up? Perhaps even as an adult, one or both parents could still be playing games. What do you think you could do to stop game playing in your family? If your parents were not game players, that is another reason for you to thank them for raising you well. Only in eulogies do some parents receive gratitude from their children. If they are still alive, you could consider expressing gratitude to them now.

Regardless of the children's age, games are never a good idea, as are other behaviors in which some parents engage. Parents should be mindful, however, that children do much better, when they have two loving, caring, and stable parents, who live with them in the same home, and they are voluntarily involved in their lives.

Interestingly, an unhealthy parent is usually the one who engages in games in a family. Even if they do so unintentionally, it is they who initiate behaviors that hurt the children. Parents have a moral responsibility to ensure that their interactions with each other and with their children are consistently positive.

Despite their shortcomings, many parents do try their hardest to raise their children well, and to guide their development into emotionally intelligent, stable, and productive adults. From this perspective, some adults applaud their parents' efforts, and they give much of the credit to them for the life that they now enjoy.

Some parents, however, never get the opportunity to feel proud of their children's accomplishments. Despite what they feel might have been their best efforts, the children sometimes think that they did a terrible job, and they blame them for whatever dysfunction or unhappiness they experienced. As we know, parenting is not an exact science. Additionally, there is no rehearsal. It is a one-shot, learn-as-you-go deal that often presents many hiccups.

Furthermore, when many parents review how they raised their children, they sometimes agree that with the knowledge they now have, if they had a second opportunity to redo things, many of their approaches would be different. Such opportunity, we know, simply does

The Role of Parents

not exist. What exists, however, is an opportunity for adults to address many concerns that they encountered in their childhood.

It is important for individuals to recognize that in addition to receiving help with concerns from their childhood, they have opportunities to process and successfully address numerous other life challenges as well. Full utilization of available resources could enable them to experience and fully understand the meanings of concepts such as acceptance, forgiveness, patience, tolerance, and cycle breaking.

Indeed, as adults, when some individuals reflect on their lives and on the roles that their parents played, they soon realize that their situation may not have been as bad as they might have once thought. Others decide to work diligently at improving themselves, and with help from trained professionals, trusted friends, and others, they have been able to triumph over their perceived weaknesses.

Life is challenging. As human beings, there are also some options, like getting to choose our parents, that we simply never had, nor can we change them. Even so, as adults, we face the enormous responsibility of deciding how we wish to forge ahead with the lives that we acquired—the only lives that we will ever have. Only we alone can make that decision. Not even our parents, who raised us, can help us with that, and neither can anyone else.

4

Living a Fulfilling Life

FOR MANY OF us, this very enigmatic life that we have been given, is seemingly continuously being bombarded with various stressors and unexpected situations. Life can be so stressful at times, that sometimes it makes some individuals wonder how they were ever able to triumph over the challenges that they faced.

Despite this observation, in many instances, life is also pleasant, beautiful, and enjoyable, to the extent that it makes some individuals wish that they could live longer to enjoy more of it. For us to live what could be considered a fulfilling life, however, one that is filled with health, happiness, success, and prosperity, many positive factors must come together in various areas of our lives, and we must be able to enjoy them fully, by ourselves and with others.

What exactly is a fulfilling life? And who determines what that should look like? Is it having many family members and friends to share life with? Is it having a life of opulence and independence? Is it having feelings of contentment, regardless of how little one has? Is it living in solitude away from others? Truthfully, because fulfillment means so many different things to different people, it could be all those things. In many instances also, it depends on one's cultural background, how they were socialized and the changes that they choose to institute.

Even within some cultures, subcultures of individuals exist, who prefer to "walk to the beats of their own drum." They reject the traditional ideas of the major culture to which they were exposed, and they opt instead to lead lives that are different. Hence, while some individuals conceptualize a fulfilling life as one that involves affluence and hedonism, others reject such views, choosing to embrace one that involves more minimalism and tranquility instead.

The problem is that although society sets guidelines in terms of how people should live their lives, not everyone conforms to those dictates. Additionally, disparities exist between various groups, which imply that broad rules and expectations are usually ineffective. Notwithstanding, from our youth, we are usually receiving messages that tell us what to do and from what to abstain.

Many variables force people to live their lives in ways that are contrary to society's rules. There is also the expectation that, regardless of who they are or where they reside, individuals should have certain basic needs met. Therefore, many individuals feel that a very important role of the government is to ensure that its citizens are provided with fundamental resources such as healthcare, education, shelter, and food.

Yet, we know that the availability and the distribution of some very basic resources are of major concern, especially in third-world countries. Indeed, even in some first-world countries, where a surplus of many supplies and services exists, homelessness, poverty, hunger, educational deficits, and the availability of basic healthcare, are still significant challenges. This makes life so overwhelmingly difficult, that mental health and other significant concerns have become widespread.

Additionally, to cope with life's ills, some individuals find themselves resorting to negative coping mechanisms, such as drug use and frequent alcohol consumption. These practices compound the situation even further, and they make the initial concerns even more difficult to address effectively.

In the absence of even the very basic amenities that people need to survive, it is difficult for many to live lives that could be considered fulfilling. Each year, billions of dollars are spent addressing problems stemming from drug addictions, alcoholism, and other significant mental health concerns. Perhaps the problems would not have been as widespread if mental health was viewed as more of a priority, and a significant amount of those funds were injected into proper preventive programs than into treatment after the fact.

But we know that fixing mental health and other related challenges is more complicated than it seems. Indeed, many serious attempts have been made to address those challenges over the years. Unfortunately, it appears that no matter how much has been done, the problem persists. In fact, with the increased stressors to which many individuals are consistently exposed daily, many reports now suggest that the problems have been getting worse.

As a seasoned psychotherapist, I am aware that many members of our society feel they have never gotten a fair shot at having a life that could be considered fulfilling. I have worked with many of those individuals over the years. It might take time to receive help. However, opportunities do exist in many areas that individuals could use to improve. More attention needs to be paid to teaching people appropriate self-help skills that they can use, especially during times of increased stress, so that they may not consider using inappropriate and self-destructive measures.

Despite the existence of opportunities to improve, many individuals find themselves in situations in which they are not aware of resources that are available, or they may not have any idea of how to access important services when they are required. Consequently, they get disillusioned, and they resort to the use of measures that are more readily available.

A practice that has become very common nowadays, is for individuals to start questioning their existence. Reports are also affirming that more people, especially younger ones, have either been considering giving up or they are taking their own lives. Since the start of the pandemic, increases in suicidal ideations and completed suicides have become significant concerns.

For one reason or another, more people seem to be feeling that they have been trying their hardest to stay afloat during these very stressful times. However, somehow, no matter what they do, improving their situation, and getting the opportunity to enjoy their lives, as so many others around them have done, always seem to elude them.

In addition to other concerns, mental health challenges, mood disorders, and anxiety disorders resulting from individuals, who feel discontented about their lives, without seemingly any way out, have become major concerns in the United States. Clearly, the situation begs for interventions that are both more urgent and effective. Unfortunately, unless such measures are put in place, suicidal ideations, suicide attempts, and suicide completions will continue to be correspondingly major concerns.

To make matters even worse, numerous barriers that are associated with help-seeking, particularly for mental health challenges, prevent many individuals from choosing to utilize services that are available, when they are required. Now that the need for more mental health services has skyrocketed during the current pandemic, greater emphasis needs to be placed on educating members of the public on the more common challenges that are being experienced, and how to secure urgent, confidential help.

Living a Fulfilling Life

It is important for individuals to be aware that if they need help, they can receive confidential assistance in many areas, twenty-four-hours-per-day, seven-days-per-week. For those who feel so overwhelmed that ending their lives seem like a possible option, they can call the **National Suicide Prevention Hotline toll free, at 1-800-273-8255**. Private therapists and community mental health agencies are also available in many areas to help individuals address challenges that they may be experiencing.

A significant development during the current pandemic, involves the more widespread use of telehealth, and especially telebehavioral health services. Regardless of where some people reside, they have been able to utilize those services privately, from within the confines of their own homes. Reports suggest that many individuals enjoy using home-based services, not only because of privacy concerns, but also because of the convenience that it also affords them.

It is true that numerous challenges exist on our planet. What is also true is that many individuals find it almost impossible to find their way on their own. It should be encouraging for them to understand that they are not unique in that regard. Although their numbers could use improvement, it's good to know that trained, experienced, competent, and empathetic professionals are available to provide help to them, and that help is also home-based.

Many individuals do not have to suffer silently anymore. Nor do they have to wait until things get so bad that they feel hopeless. While it is true that many mental health challenges have become more common in the United States, what is equally true is that many individuals who once felt the same way as others might be feeling, have received help and they are now enjoying their lives. They are now living lives that are far more fulfilling.

Even so, historically, stigma and mistrust have been associated with help-seeking, and especially with mental health care. Therefore, even with the increased demand for services, unless they are in a crisis or they are ordered to do so by the courts, some Americans are still reluctant to get help.

Fortunately, more widely available internet services also imply that information is more accessible than it used to be. This has enabled some individuals to develop greater awareness, to make more informed decisions, and even to employ better self-help measures.

In recent years, in their attempts to improve themselves, many Americans have been turning to the use of self-help books and social media sites, where they can secure information privately. As a result, some individuals are more knowledgeable and more vocal about conditions that affect them and measures that they might have used to help themselves.

In many ways, these trends could be viewed in positive terms. Notwithstanding, there are negative concerns as well. In some cases, greater access to information could lead to wrong self-diagnoses, increased anxiety, and even to self-harm. In many cases, access to information is not the problem. Rather, it is the use of the information to which individuals are exposed that can become problematic.

Take the case with depression for example. All kinds of information about depression symptoms, assessments, diagnostic tools, and treatments are available online. Yet, while it is good to be aware of the various aspects of depression, some types of information in untrained and unprofessional hands can be worrisome for many vulnerable individuals. To receive the best possible care, they should ensure that they balance self-knowledge with professional consultation.

Common symptoms of depression can be found at the website for the Centers for Disease Control and Prevention (CDC), but they are not meant for individuals to engage in self-diagnoses. Rather, they are outlined for educational purposes, to help individuals decide if they might be dealing with situations that warrant consultation with trained medical or mental health professionals.

Not only can trained medical or mental health professionals assist individuals with appropriate diagnoses, but also, they can suggest appropriate treatment protocols and follow-up care if needed. Common symptoms of depression listed by the CDC (cdc.gov) include the following:

- Feeling sad or anxious often or all the time,
- Not wanting to engage in activities that they used to enjoy,
- Feeling irritable, easily frustrated, or restless,
- Having trouble falling asleep or staying asleep,
- Waking up too early or sleeping too much,
- Eating more or less than usual or having no appetite,
- Having aches, pains, headaches, or stomach problems that do not improve with treatment,

Living a Fulfilling Life

- Having trouble concentrating, remembering details, or making decisions,
- Feeling tired even after sleeping well,
- Feeling guilty, worthless, or helpless,
- Thinking about suicide or hurting others.

Life is very difficult for many individuals. Unfortunately, because it prevents some individuals from living fulfilling lives, it is also more difficult for them than it is for others.

No matter how difficult life gets, it is important for us to remember that the topography of life is not consistently even, anywhere on the planet. In fact, although perhaps not as often, even the more affluent among us, have times also when they experience their peaks and their valleys. The only difference is that they have greater access to resources, which prevents them from being as stuck as others might find themselves.

My goal for this chapter is to let individuals know, regardless of the challenges that they might now face, very rarely is the situation permanent. Everyone does have the right to live a fulfilling life. In the pursuit of that undertaking, however, help is sometimes a necessity, and it is available for individuals to accomplish their goals.

When individuals find themselves in situations that are less than desirable, they should not allow themselves to remain there until they feel immobilized. They should recognize that they do have an obligation to improve, and that they can get help to put themselves in much better positions. In the end, regardless of the outcome, one should be able to say, "I found myself in an undesirable situation, I sought help, I made the changes that were necessary, and I gave it my best." They should also try to remember that doing nothing or remaining in that state and complaining are never good options.

Following are suggestions that could be considered when thinking about living a fulfilling life:

- Develop a code by which you would like to live and stick with it.
- Surround yourself with positive and supportive people who value you.
- Prepare yourself for the future. Find a profession or a job that you really enjoy.
- Love yourself, but love others also and love them intensely.
- Learn a new language.
- Learn to play a musical instrument.

Living a Fulfilling Life

- Make time for yourself daily.
- Get adequate exercise, rest, and sleep.
- Meditate for at least 20 minutes twice daily.
- If you are religious, find time to pray.
- Develop a sense of humor. Learn to laugh at yourself. Don't take yourself too seriously.
- Always give your best.
- If you can't find something to give, give of your time.
- Help others, especially those who are in less advantageous situations than yourself.
- Find ways to express gratitude.
- Respect others, and never compromise your own self-respect.
- Show love and appreciation for your parents. If nothing else, they gave you your life.
- Learn to forgive yourself. Learn to forgive others also.
- Travel—explore the planet. There is a whole world out there just waiting for you.
- Learn to listen to yourself. Learn to listen to others also.
- Learn at least one poem and a nursery rhyme. Learn to recite them well.

- Learn a few good jokes and practice how to tell them well.
- Learn to cook at least two full-course meals.
- Enjoy yourself. Sing and dance. You may not do them well. Do them anyway. Have fun.
- Read books on a variety of subjects, or listen to them.
- Make friends. Be a good friend to at least Three people. Have both young and old friends.
- Politely greet others. Recognize them. Demonstrate that they are visible, and they do matter.
- Compliment others. Find something nice to say and be genuine about it.
- Smile. It doesn't have to be too often, but just smile.
- Make somebody's day by doing or saying something that they didn't expect.
- Find something to believe in, and believe in yourself and your own capabilities.
- When you are down, don't stay down for too long. Get right back up and keep going.
- Treat yourself well.

Living a Fulfilling Life

- Be approachable. Be someone people want to be around.
- Learn a new hobby or skill and practice it. Be good at it. Enjoy it.
- Be kind to animals.
- Keep your surroundings clean.
- Save—no matter how small. Sometimes it is difficult, but unless you have access to unlimited funds, learn not to splurge.
- Know where important resources are located and how to access them when they are needed.
- Don't be afraid to ask for help.
- Learn how to say "No," but learn to say "Yes," at least sometimes.
- Learn to apologize when you are wrong.
- Keep your promises, especially those that you made to yourself.
- Find ways to motivate and encourage those who feel unmotivated or discouraged.
- Words can hurt. Remember to think before you speak.
- Be kind to strangers. You never know what role they could play in your life in the future.

- Learn not to criticize others. They are just as imperfect as you are.
- Make sure you own at least one full length mirror. It never lies.
- If you are going to dream, dream big.
- Practice being honest with yourself. It could make it much harder for you to lie to others.
- Appreciate what you have. Do not focus your energies on acquiring things that you don't have, on things that you lost, or on things that are not very important.
- People will tell you to look in the windscreen instead of the rearview mirror. It is good to glance in the rearview mirror occasionally, because not only bad things happened in the past. Good things happened there also. It is okay to focus on the good things that occurred in the past. They helped shape who you are today. Make sure you never forget them.
- Remember those who helped you, especially during your roughest moments.
- Invest in your physical health and in your mental health also.

Living a Fulfilling Life

- Live, so that at any point in your life you can honestly say, "I did my best."
- Be your true self. Be authentic.
- Learn to accept that things don't always work out the way you expect them to, nor within the timeframe that you would like. Learn to be okay with both.
- When things get rough, and sometimes they will, remember you have a history of surviving rough times. Try to recall some survival resources that were used in the past. Use them again.
- Remember, nothing lasts, not the good times, nor the bad ones either.
- Remember, you will not always win. You will not always lose either.
- Find something to celebrate in your own life and celebrate things with others in theirs.
- At midday, be grateful that you made it through the morning. Before you go to sleep at night, give thanks for making it through the evening. Give thanks for making it through another day.
- Each day, find someone to thank for helping you with something during that day.
- Constantly go out of your way to help others.

- Remove words like, "I don't know," "I can't," or "I will try" from your vocabulary. Instead, say, "I will look into it, or "I will do it."
- Learn to keep your cool. Loudness, anxiety, and anger are all peace robbers.
- Take responsibility for your behavior, and never allow anyone to decide how you behave.
- You cannot avoid stress, but you can learn to manage it well.
- It is not how gregarious you are but the depth of your relationships that matters.
- Never get involved in your parent's disagreements and never take the side of one parent over the other.
- Live your life in moderation. Too much of anything is usually problematic.
- Count your blessings. Focus on them, especially when things don't seem to be going well.
- Always find ways to give back. If you think you've never received anything, consider how much you brought with you when you came into the world.
- Learn to shelter from the rain. It's not getting wet that you should be afraid of, it's the lightning.

Living a Fulfilling Life

- As much as you can, prepare for natural disasters. They do occur, and if you are not prepared, they can be disastrous.
- Listen to older folks. Their memory might fade as they age, but with age does come wisdom.
- When playing games with children, don't let them always lose. Allow them to win sometimes. They may not understand how they won, but think about the lessons they can learn about winning and losing.
- You only have one body and one mind. Remember, your input will determine the output.
- Before sharing personal information with children, think about the lesson(s) that you would like them to learn and whether the information will help them become better people.
- If you told someone a lie, you should find a way to make amends by disclosing the truth. It is better to be punished and be forgiven for lying than to live a phony life.

5

What Matters in the End?

I SPENT THE greater part of the past six decades looking at my life and pondering many of the same ideas as my readers. Who am I? Why am I here? What have the roles of my parents been in my life? Am I living a fulfilling life? And, finally, In the end, what really matters?

Disappointingly, I have yet to find answers to any of those questions. This does not necessarily mean that none among us hasn't. Perhaps, there are individuals who do have answers, and I would love to meet at least one such person, who has gained some insight into those matters. I know I would enjoy having meaningful conversations with them and I would also have much to learn. Even so, however intelligent someone might be, and regardless of whatever claims they might make, I remain skeptical that any such person exists.

My quest for greater knowledge about life and its meaning began before I was even seven years old, when I lost my younger brother, who died suddenly. He was only a year younger than me, and I have never forgotten him. I know my life would have been very different, if he had not exited so early. I cannot say for sure how much different it would have been, but one thing I do know is that it was from then that the serious questions about life started to emerge.

By the time I was twenty years old, I lost a younger sister, an older sister, my mother, several aunts and uncles, cousins, and very close friends. What I have now come to realize is that, regardless of one's age, when people, who are very close to you start dying, one after the other, it makes you start to wonder about important matters, like whether your time could be coming up soon.

What makes things more complicated, is not having someone who you trust, who could have those honest and very deep conversations with you about life and its meaning. Someone, who could voluntarily sit you down and provide you with simple, age-appropriate explanations when strange phenomena like illnesses and death invariably occur in your life.

In the absence of any kind of conversation about such matters, many individuals, old and young alike, are forced to continue very bravely to live their lives, as if they are left unscathed by those strange and inexplicable

What Matters in the End?

occurrences. When they are very young, many children learn to pretend that they understand mundane happenings, and that their lives are just as "normal" as everyone else's. Well, we know that quite often that is simply just not the case. That was the situation in which I also found myself.

I was forced to try to figure out things for myself, or to conduct my own searches about whatever situations I did not understand. I couldn't understand, for example, why my younger brother would choose to go away to heaven, as I was told, without taking me with him, or why he never returned. We were used to going almost everywhere together and wherever we went, we always returned.

Neither could I understand why my neighbor kept beating his wife almost every week. I thought, surely, she must have been giving him a great deal of trouble and that was how he disciplined her. They were about the same size. I could not wrap my mind around why she would just take the beatings without ever fighting back. I did get some explanations, mainly from eavesdropping on adult conversations. However, even today, many of those explanations remain incredibly unacceptable to me.

Flawed though they may have been, I developed my own ideas about diverse life experiences, and I would knowledgeably and boastfully promote them to my peers, many of whom bought into them and made me feel like I was a genius. As I look back now, I realize that those were the early beginnings of my counseling career. Even some of the older neighbors used to seek my counsel, and the more I practiced, the better I seemed to become at it.

Nevertheless, I am the first to admit that I know I have never had the luxury of what some children could describe as a "normal" life. In many cases, while they were looking forward to achieving various milestones in their lives, and to enjoying birthday parties and other celebrations, I spent much of my early years thinking about death and dying and other occurrences that I thought were strange, even for many adults.

Sometimes, I think I was robbed of a normal childhood, because of the many significant traumatic events to which I was exposed. Even so, I often find solace in the idea that, if things were otherwise, if they were more normal, I would never have been able to seek the trainings that were necessary for me to develop greater understanding and put myself in a position in which

What Matters in the End?

I have been able to empathetically help so many other individuals.

Some of my friends find it strange when I share with them that there was a long time when I didn't even remember my own birthday. It just was not something that was ever celebrated or even remembered. In fact, it was not until I was in my thirties, and I migrated to the United States, that I had my first birthday celebration.

I didn't know anything about the Tooth Fairy, about Saint Valentine, or Santa Claus either. I remember learning of those characters in books, or I heard people talking about them. However, they were never a part of my experiences growing up, not even into my early adult years. Therefore, I could not relate to them. Not surprisingly, my attitude toward many traditions that some people celebrate, or that they take for granted, is still far different from theirs.

For one thing, nowhere on the island of my native Jamaica, have I ever seen a house with a chimney or a fireplace. It is a tropical island. Maybe there are some in certain areas, but I just have never seen them. Plus, I don't see the need for chimneys or fireplaces there. Neither have I ever met Santa Claus or anyone else from the North Pole. I don't think Santa ever visited Jamaica when I was growing up. He must have stopped in North America, in Florida. He certainly did not visit children in the countryside where I grew up, because I would have at least heard about it.

At Christmastime, we had the best foods to eat. I think every family in Jamaica did. Sometimes they would make special preparations just for that festive season. But we didn't waste money that we could have used to buy other more important things, on a tree that we would dress-up and then throw it away soon after. I know some people who did cut down trees, any type of tree, and they would put lights on them. But even those occurrences were very rare. Additionally, we never had electricity in my neighborhood when I was growing up. So, where would the lights come from?

Yet those were "normal" Christmases for me as they were for my friends (Some did get presents, but my brothers and I learned to make our own toys, with which we had a great deal of fun). We didn't know anything different. Nor did we think we were missing out on anything. Even more importantly, today, we are not any worse off than anyone else who was raised with different experiences in other parts of Jamaica or even in first-world countries.

What Matters in the End?

Unless I tell those stories today, no one would even suspect the possibilities of such unique experiences. Yet, in my own mind, I have had a very challenging, but still a very normal and enjoyable life. Even if I could trade my life for another, even if things could be any different, I would not be interested. I have learned to be very content with my life.

Those experiences molded me into the person I am today. Not only do I love my life, I also love my parents, my siblings, my relatives, my friends, and all the life experiences that I have gained. I have learned valuable lessons from even the bad experiences as well. So, I have come to appreciate the good things and even some of the not-so-good ones that occurred over the past six decades of my existence. Without them, what my life might have been like, is simply unfathomable.

The circumstances under which I was raised, and the experiences to which I was exposed, forced me to develop some of my own explanations about life, about people, and about the world in which we live. In many cases also, they may not make much sense to others. But they make sense to me, and they help bring me peace of mind. From my vantage point, my life is like none other. This reinforces in me the idea that we are all unique. My way of being works for me and it must. The onus is on everyone else to understand their ways of being and to make who they are work for them.

In the end, does it all matter? Does anything really matter? Will it just be over? Will it just be as if nothing ever took place? Will all that we have done be for naught? Do we all just go from being to non-being? It is very difficult to conceptualize. Some individuals are not even willing to entertain discussions about the subject, because it is too existential and too anxiety-provoking.

I know that in my own small way, through the services that I provide, I continue to touch many lives. It is also with a great sense of humility that I acknowledge the frequency with which I am reminded of the significant differences that I continue to make in the world. But I do not practice my profession for a reward. In fact, providing psychotherapy is very stressful at times.

Additionally, one thing about being a therapist is that no matter how good the performance, no matter how outstanding the interactions with others, therapists do not get stars on the Hollywood Walk of Fame. Nor do they get Oscars, Emmys, or Grammys. Those are designated for performers and entertainers, who provide other seemingly more significant services. Therapists are not

What Matters in the End?

adequately remunerated either. Many therapists must learn how to find satisfactory supplemental compensation in other ways.

I have been providing counseling and therapeutic-type services for a significant part of my life, and I am convinced that it has something to do with my purpose. I have worked in other fields before I decided to become a therapist, and I could have been doing many other things presently. But providing counseling services is such a natural fit for me, that oftentimes I find myself saying that I didn't choose to become a therapist. The profession chose me.

I am reminded by others very frequently that it is not a profession that everyone finds suitable. Not everyone naturally possesses the patience, the tolerance and the empathetic characteristics and other skills that the profession demands, and some things simply cannot be taught.

I know that what I do is very important. I know that individuals who decide to share their lives with me are very important and very courageous as well and I never take the opportunity to interact with them and to share in their lives lightly. Still, the burning question remains. In the end, after I cease to exist, will what I did matter? To whom will it matter? Who will ever call my name in twenty, fifty or seventy-five years after I die? I see what happens to other individuals just like me. Who do you think will remember you? Who will be calling your name?

Many individuals do not like to have conversations about this subject, because it reminds them too much of their own mortality, which is exactly what we are talking about. But I realize that even when they refuse to engage in that type of conversation, quite often it is still very much on their minds. How can they escape it? Sooner or later, it is something that happens to all of us.

The final question on the January 2022 survey on life that was conducted online asked respondents whether they thought their existence would matter in the end. Only about 13 percent said no. The other almost 87 percent responded with a resounding yes! Certainly, this is a matter that could benefit from further exploration.

Yet, this situation leads to even more questions that could be considered of equal importance. For one thing, what would make most individuals feel that they, or what they do throughout their lives matter in the end? What evidence, if any, do they have that would support their positions? Could those in the majority all be wrong?

What Matters in the End?

Could those in the minority be right? What do those in the minority have that would support their positions?

What could be the possible implications in either case? If you believe nothing matters in the end, is it okay to live your life with reckless abandon? If you feel it does matter, is there a certain way in which you should be living your life? This is where I believe religion can play a major role.

Even so, as imperfect, and as mistake prone as human beings are, unless significant allowances are in place for making mistakes and for wrongdoing, it doesn't seem possible for anyone to be able to lead a life that would still guarantee them rewards for their inconsistently good actions. Are human beings capable of being good consistently? What about those who find that perfection is unattainable? Are there really guarantees of forgiveness and allowances for redemption? How about those who are habitual wrongdoers? Are they doomed?

Many individuals try to answer these questions, if they get seriously ill, or if they live until they are old. They usually make major behavioral changes, sometimes-even at great sacrifice, before their expiration date inevitably arrives, especially if they thought they were not on track before.

But there are those among us, who believe in the existence of a Book of Life. They feel that the Universe keeps indelible records of all our activities, and that at some point, there will be a reckoning. Some religious individuals find this idea scary because they recognize how very difficult it is to live a life that is pure. The idea that one, by their very imperfect nature, cannot have a perfect record, but they will still be chastised for their imperfections, is enough to increase their level of anxiety.

One thing I have come to realize is that no matter how much we might try to deny its existence or to disguise our feelings about it, we humans have seemingly unhealthy relationships with endings, especially as they pertain to our own demise. And, as if talking about it, or worse yet, preparing for it, would make it occur sooner, many of us are not willing to engage in any meaningful discourse about it either.

Some teenagers get very anxious when they realize their adolescent years are about to end. Some individuals, who are getting married, look forward to their change in status. Still, although they are in love and they are about to start their own independent lives, and their own families, sometimes they get cold feet from the realization that their lives as singles are ending. On the odd

What Matters in the End?

occasion, some individuals even cancel their wedding, or they don't show up. The thought of giving up singlehood, their liberty, and their independence, is far too scary. They finally come to the realization that they are not as ready for matrimonial life as they may have thought.

When some people become parents, although they do love the idea of having children and of bringing new life into the world, some secretly think about their lives as individuals, that they are about to give up, forever. Then there is the case with divorce. Just as losing a loved one through death, divorce is one of the biggest stressors in a person's life. Individuals are known to go through the same stages of grieving when they divorce, as when someone close dies. The effects of both, usually affect many individuals, for the rest of their lives.

Insofar as the fear of endings is concerned, I feel it is pointless to worry about it. After all, nothing lasts. Everything is impermanent. Moreover, I believe that remaining cognizant of the inevitable nature of the ending of life can help us live in a more fulfilling manner.

In my role as a psychotherapist, some of the most important lessons that I have had the opportunity to learn about life, or rather the end of life, were from individuals who were dying. Some of those individuals were my clients. So, I cannot share details of conversations that transpired between us. I am also not willing to share details of conversations that I had with other individuals who are still alive, even if I obtained their permission to do so, unless, in my judgment, the information could be significantly beneficial to others.

Following are scenarios that occurred recently with two individuals who I knew very well. The first was my youngest brother, Kenneth, who died in July 2019 in Jamaica, and the other was a close friend.

My brother had been in the hospital for about a week, and he was not improving. His prognosis was also guarded. Just months before, my younger sister (his older sister) had died, as did my oldest brother, who resided in the Central American country of Belize. So, I had three significant losses within only months of each other.

Although more than a decade my junior, my brother and I had always been inexpressibly close. I guess I had always seen him as a fitting replacement for my other younger brother, who had died many years before he was born.

Not only did my brother look up to me, and he saw me as his mentor, but also, because he was aware that I had very high expectations of him. I think he lived with

What Matters in the End?

the fear that he might have done something to disappoint me at some point, and I would have somehow not found it possible to forgive him. That never happened.

While hospitalized, my brother and I spoke daily. The conversations were usually about how he was feeling, whether he was in pain, what the doctors were saying, how they were planning to treat his condition, and what they thought about his prognosis. He tried to reassure me that I should not worry, but honestly, I didn't see how I couldn't. I was very concerned. I could never get satisfactory answers from him, and medical personnel were never there to provide answers when I called. Of my eight siblings, only two of them were still alive, and deep in my soul I felt like I was on the verge of losing another one.

Then, on the eighth night of his hospitalization, just before 10:30 PM, the following text message was on my phone:

"My dearest brother, Percy. I hope you are doing well, and you are not there in America worrying about me. I feel very peaceful now, and I am not in any more pain. I am here thinking about you and the many positive ways in which you touched my life over the years. I thought I would use this time to write you a little thank you note. I want you to know that you are the person that cared about me the most in my entire life. You are not just a good brother. You are a good person. You showed me nothing but love and kindness. I cannot find one negative thing to say about you. You set the bar very high for me and you always set good examples for me to follow. Everything that I have become in this life, is because of you. I love you from the bottom of my heart. Although I never said it to you before, I am the luckiest person in the world to have a brother like you. I couldn't ask for anything more. I don't think I have much longer to live, and I don't want you to be sad. You have done enough for me. Please take care of yourself and your family and I hope we will see each other again."

At 2:17 AM, I got up to use the bathroom and I checked my messages to see if there was anything important or urgent before going back to sleep. His mesage was the only one on my phone. I read it and I cried uncontrollably for about ten minutes. Then I called

What Matters in the End?

his number. The phone rang almost incessantly for about seven minutes. Finally, my niece answered. "He is gone," she said, crying. "Uncle Kenneth died at about 11:15 last night. I have his phone." I was speechless. Somehow, I suspected. However, I was not ready for the confirmation. Not so soon.

"I didn't get to hear his voice again," I thought. Not only did I have to process all the memories that were associated with our lives, but also, even with everything else that I was enduring with my own health challenges and with the recent death of my sister and my oldest brother, I had another trip to make, and another funeral to plan. Plus, I was in the middle of a very nasty divorce after a twenty-nine-year marriage.

It did not take me too long to stop feeling sorry for myself. I had no time for self-pity or to process my own emotions. I had to be on the next flight to Kingston, even if it would be just for the weekend. I had to return to Florida very hastily, because my divorce hearing was on the following Tuesday. I went to Jamaica as planned, I made final arrangements for my brother's funeral, which I could not have attended, and I returned to Florida. On Tuesday morning, I went to my divorce hearing, and Wednesday night I checked myself into the emergency room at the local hospital. I had just lost three of my siblings, I was not feeling well, and I was alone.

We are now addressing the topic of what matters in the end. Each time I read my brother's text, which I still have, I ask myself many questions. Was that what mattered to him in the end? Why did he not call me instead, so that I could hear his voice one more time? At what point did he realize he was facing the end? I have faced situations dealing with death so many times throughout my life that there are dozens of others on which I could have chosen to focus. Let's be clear though, what end are we talking about? Is it the physical end of those who are gone and the end of the relationship that existed between them and those who are still alive?

I would be the first to adamantly disagree that one's relationship with another person ends at death. I still think of my brother, almost daily. I also think about my grandparents, my parents, my other siblings, aunts and uncles, friends, coworkers, some of my clients, and many others. In this regard, I am very thankful that my memory is still intact. Having a good memory, and recalling positive things about our deceased loved ones, do keep them alive. So, in the end, do they matter? Did my relationship with them matter? Should I try to forget

What Matters in the End?

about them now and just get on with my life? It simply does not work that way.

I have such fond memories of so many individuals who have died, that I simply refuse to just let them go. In fact, now I am at the stage in my life, where I have many more loved ones, who are dead than the number that I have who are still alive, and, through the good memories that I have of them, I maintain very strong connections with them.

While I am alive and my memory is still intact, so too will they be alive. When I am alone, I can decide which memories I wish to recall, and how I wish to feel. Sometimes, I close my eyes, as I do my recall, or at other times I review pictures in one of the many photo albums that I keep. Some individuals think it is strange, and they try not to remember those who are gone already.

But this is my life. Each person with whom I was close, was a part of it for a reason. I cannot voluntarily choose to forget about them, because although physically they are no longer here, the memories that we shared are still with me. Individuals who have experiences with the death of their loved ones know exactly what I am talking about.

Still, I know some people who go even further when it comes to the memories of their loved ones. They keep urns with their ashes if they were cremated, they put some of the ashes in lockets that they wear as pendants, or they visit their gravesites with flowers and have conversations, as if they are still there. Truthfully, memories of loved ones and how they are revered are very personal. No one has the right to say how those matters should be handled.

In many situations, I find something, or I remember an important circumstance from the past that reminds me of someone, and I express the appropriate emotions at that time. Sometimes it's with tears, other times it is with a smile, or at other times it is with uncontrollable laughter. I do as I see fit. This does not imply in any way that there is a focus on the past or that an obsession exists with those who have died. Surely, they may have died, but their memories will last, as long as I do.

In any case, as a professional helper, most of my life today is spent in conversations with individuals, who are struggling to cope with the vicissitudes of their daily lives. So, when I am with others, I do not have time to reflect on those who are deceased. Rather, occasional reminders may arise in the form of a song, a familiar statement, a smell, or an idea, which brings back a particular memory. I do attend a bereavement group once weekly.

What Matters in the End?

The second situation that I will mention pertains to a friend, David (not his real name). He was so jovial that, at times, it was challenging for others to be serious for a long time, when he was present. He could make light of any situation, and indeed he did. Primarily because of the lighter energy that he brought to many situations; numerous individuals found him particularly likable. I knew he was battling something. However, Jamaican men are knowingly tight-lipped about their health challenges. He didn't volunteer any information, and I refused to pry.

I always felt like at some point, if he wanted me to know and he felt comfortable enough, he would tell me what was going on. Finally, one morning, he mustered up enough courage to tell me what was going on. For some reason, I got the impression that he had forgotten about my background in Public Health. So, he was rather impressed, it seemed, with my knowledge about his condition, when we finally talked. It appeared to have given him the impetus to converse with me much further.

There is such a major difference between growing up in rural Jamaica and living in the United States. In the United States, one just does not get time to hang out with friends or even with relatives, as they were accustomed to on the island. Consequently, people could reside near to each other, and they may even converse with one another on the telephone regularly. Only some, however, spend time with each other, especially when they are in relatively new relationships, or when they are raising families.

In my youth, most homes in rural Jamaica did not have telephones. This implied that one did not have the luxury of calling a friend to say that they were going to visit. One would just turn up at their friend's house, and it was okay. In the United States, life is very different. People are very busy. In many cases also, hanging out with friends or engaging in certain other types of social activities, just naturally get placed on the back burner. Otherwise, they have a way of making relationships more complicated than they usually can be already. Many men share that oftentimes they would like to hang out more with friends. However, they are concerned about the backlash from their wives.

I did not see David very often. Then, on one unusually busy Wednesday afternoon I received a telephone call from him. I recognized his voice immediately. Plus, his name came up on the caller identification on my phone. I had just returned from lunch with friends, and my next client would not have been until 1:30 PM.

"Percy," he said. "How are you?" "I am good," I replied. "It's good to hear from you." "We have not seen each other in quite a while. Did you move?" "No," he replied. "I still live at the same house. Can you come see me?" "Come see you?" I responded. "Come see you where?" "I am in the hospital," he replied. "In the hospital? What's up? "When you come, I will explain," he said." "Give me a few hours and I will be there," I told him. "I have a couple people to see. Then I will come. Which hospital, and what is your room number?" I asked him. He told me the name of the hospital and his room number. "See you shortly. I am looking forward to seeing you. I have not had any visitors in a while." "Ok. See you soon," I responded.

With the permission of my final patient, who I asked to be rescheduled, and she agreed, I left my office at about 3:15 PM for the hospital. I did not know what to expect. Over the years, I visited many individuals, both family members and friends, at that same hospital, but for some reason, this time I had a nervous feeling in my stomach that things were going to be quite different.

A gift that I know I've had for many years, is the ability to look beyond what individuals present and see their essence, if you will. Who they really are. I used to think that was how everyone operated, but it was not until I became a therapist that I realized that it is not the case at all. Little did I know that more than ever before, I would need those skills that evening.

I have learned not to put too much emphasis on appearances. Containers are changeable and temporary. I have practiced focusing my attention more on the deeper, more imperceptible but enduring, inner utterances, on what a person might not be saying, using words.

When I walked into the room, I did not recognize David because of all of the weight he had lost. He smiled, very awkwardly, but I have been around enough individuals who were severely ill to understand how difficult the situation probably is for them, and how careful I must be about what I say and how I behave. It is not about me at all. It is all about them.

I dug very deeply in my soul to maintain my composure, to hold back the tears. He was noticeably very ill. What would I be crying for anyway? I am not the one in the bed. I wasn't experiencing any pain or discomfort. I reminded myself that I was there in a supportive role, and anything that I did, must reflect that. I didn't even know what was going on yet.

What Matters in the End?

"Do you need me to do anything?" I enquired. Is there anything I can do that would make you feel comfortable?" He replied, "Just sit on the bed beside me, and if you don't mind, can you hold my hand and listen to me please?" Without hesitating, I complied. Honestly, I did wonder whether I should ask for a mask and gloves. However, at that moment I did not consider any risks.

"I am dying," he said. "I have cancer, and I don't have much time left. You are my friend and I trust you. That's why I called you. I am asking you to do some very important things for me, urgently." "Sure," I said. "Just tell me what you need." I looked into his eyes, and I listened very intently to every word that he said. His intelligence was still intact. His words were very direct and sensible. I have never, nor will I ever repeat what he asked me to do. They were his personal wishes and he trusted me enough to make the requests of me.

My skills as a seasoned therapist were very helpful at that moment. I listened without interrupting him once. Moreover, his requests were so straightforward, that there wasn't any need for further explanation or clarification. His hand was so cold! I had never felt anything like that before. Then he said, "I know my hand is cold, but just continue to hold it. Your hand is warm, and when I close my eyes, it reminds me that I am not alone. I don't want to die alone. Please stay with me."

He held on to my hand very tightly, and then he cried out loudly in pain. I said to him, "Would you like me to call the nurse for you? Maybe she could give you some more Morphine." "No," he replied. "I am getting the maximum dose. It's not working anymore" Then he gave me a very detailed description of what the pain felt like and how unbearable it was. From his description and with my very vivid imagination, it's as if I could feel it myself. I tried not to say much, and I didn't ask many questions.

"It's ok to ask me questions, you know," he said, with what looked like a smile. Although now I wondered whether it was just perimortem facial muscular activity. "Are you afraid," I asked. "Hell, yes!" he said with a surprising chuckle. "You see all the things we always hear about dying, I have not experienced any of them, at least not yet. Maybe that will come later, but I just wish the pain would go away, that it would just end."

Intermittently, he would open his eyes for a while, and, without blinking, he would give that very long and intense stare that I used to hear old folks in Jamaica call

What Matters in the End?

"traveling." It was as if he was looking out for miles, and nothing could break his gaze.

"Would you like to tell me anything else now?" I asked, "Or, would you just like to rest?" "Give me a minute," he said. Soon after, he asked me to give him some jelly that was in a small container on his nightstand. Then he asked me for some ice chips. I did as he requested. Then he asked me to read something to him, which I did. This was one of the most humbling moments of my entire life. It was an opportunity for me to perform the ultimate service to someone, I told myself.

From that experience, I developed an even deeper sense of respect for nurses and for what they do, especially hospice nurses who care for those who are terminally ill, and they are in their final moments. I thought about the importance of service to others, and how fragile and unpredictable life is. I thought about what it will be like for me when my turn comes. Will I also be alone? Will I be in severe and unbearable pain? Who will I call? What will be my final wishes?

That evening, I stayed with David until about 2:30 AM. Although I wished I could have remained longer, the reality was that I was tired. I was physically and emotionally drained. If I was going to be able to see the patients that I had on my schedule later that morning, or if I was going to be able to return to see David later that evening, I had to make sure that I recharged my own batteries. I had to get some much needed and well-deserved rest. Leaving was necessary, but it was also very difficult.

I told him that I was going home, but I would be back that evening. I remembered his words, when he asked me to "hold his hands," because he did not "want to die alone." Each time I thought about leaving, all kinds of thoughts came to mind. While I was there, no one came to see him, and no one called. Was he going to die soon? Would it be that morning after I left? Would he be alone? What else could I do?

Even in those moments, he was very understanding. "Go get some rest." He said. "But make sure you come back later. I will still be here. I am not going anywhere yet. And when you are coming, bring me a cupcake from the deli." "Sure," I replied. "Any particular flavor?" "No," he responded. "I just feel in the mood for something sweet." "No problem," I said. Then I went to use the restroom. I went back to say goodnight, and I left.

That was one of the most remarkable experiences of my entire life, and it is one that I will never forget. When I got to my car, I sat there for what seemed like another few hours, processing everything. Then I cried. I am not sure whether I was upset because he was there alone, or if it was the entire situation.

I was so exhausted that I decided to take the rest of that day off. I was in no condition to see anyone that day. Later that morning, I went into my office. I called all my patients that I had scheduled, and I asked them to reschedule for alternate times. Gratefully, no one was in crisis, and the exercise went very well.

I made sure I ate well, I meditated, and I slept for a few hours. I returned to the hospital at about 5:30 PM that evening. When I arrived, I was greeted by one of David's very close friends from college, Peter (not his real name). Peter was more like a brother to him, and he was a champion caregiver. Everyone deserves to have at least one friend like Peter. I learned that he had taken David to the hospital, and he was instrumental in taking care of him during the time before he called me.

Peter and I exchanged pleasantries, but we couldn't help but notice the awkward tension in the room. So much was not being said. So much would never be said. "Thank God," I thought. "I know how to self-soothe, how to deflect from my own feelings and focus on the reason we were there—to provide comfort and support for David, during his time of need.

That evening, I learned from the nurse that David had suffered two strokes earlier and that he was no longer talking. He did regain some speech. However, it was difficult to understand what he was saying. We just had to listen more keenly, and we asked him to blink or squeeze our hands to answer questions. One blink was "yes," two blinks were "no." One squeeze was "yes," two squeezes were "no." It worked.

My visits with David continued for a few more days, until the decision was taken to provide care for him in a formal hospice setting, which was some distance away. In my heart, I knew that it was an ending I was dealing with, and I had the arduous task of processing the recent activities, carrying out his final wishes, meeting the needs of others, and getting on with my life. It was a life that was changing, again. Each time someone close dies, one's life changes. The circle shrinks, and life is never the same. Everyone close plays a role in your life. Without them in your life, it is simply not the same. All you are left with are the memories.

Early the following morning after he was transferred to the new hospice location, when my phone beeped at

What Matters in the End?

4:47 AM, I just had a feeling that it was about him. As I got up and answered the phone, his wife said, "I hope I didn't wake you. David passed away a short while ago." "Thanks for letting me know," I said. "How are you doing? Is there anything I can do to help?" "I will call you later," she said. "To talk about the arrangements." "Okay," I said.

During the ensuing days, things became rather complicated. Numerous other unrelated events occurred, and I decided that I would not attend the funeral service. What mattered to me was the time that I spent with him before he died, not whatever would happen afterwards. Peter and I are still in touch with each other. We still have not had a conversation about David. Life goes on.

I feel fortunate that David trusted me enough to call me when he did and that I was able to help him. In the end, it must have mattered to him and it mattered to me also. I have lost many of my peers over the years. One thing I have come to realize is that we all deal with death and dying very differently. Nonetheless, whether we like it or not, whether we are ready to deal with it or not, it is something that each of us must face.

Primarily because I have had so many opportunities to deal with death, I have developed my own ways of conceptualizing it, of coping with it, and of addressing it with others. I also have a much better understanding of many things that I believe do matter in the end, and a long list of other things that just don't make the list. Surely, in the end, things that one individual may feel are important, may differ from those that another person might feel are unquestionably so.

Yet, it should be made very clear that when we talk about what really matters in the end, we must realize that at the very end, nothing really matters. What's important is what we did while we were alive and how we chose to live.

Last-minute activities in which we engage, things we start to do when we realize that we are getting older, when we feel time is running out, when we are seriously ill, or when we know that we are facing our inescapable demise, simply may not matter either. Logically, we can only think as humans do. So, who would we be trying to fool, when, toward the end, we try to play catch up? I am not sure if all our guilt-ridden feelings will matter. Again, we can only speculate.

Yet, there seems to be consensus regarding some things that may not matter at the end and some things that absolutely do. Those that many suggest may matter, include the following:

What Matters in the End?

- How much happiness we experienced.
- Kindness/helpfulness/how often and how well we served others.
- Lovingness—how many people we loved and how we expressed love.
- Patience.
- Conscientiousness.
- Having a good sense of humor.
- Politeness/respectfulness.
- Gratefulness.
- Faithfulness.
- Tolerance/being nonjudgmental of others/wanting the best for others.
- Flexibility.
- Honesty/trustworthiness.
- Empathy.
- Reliability.
- Calmness and our ability to self-soothe.
- Thoughtfulness/our investment in understanding others.
- Bravery.
- Loyalty.
- Resilience/resourcefulness.
- Courageousness.

- Truthfulness.
- Enthusiasm.
- Ambitiousness.
- Humility.
- Approachability.
- Strength/Self-confidence/tenaciousness.
- Authenticity/who we were/not who we pretended to be.
- Being a good listener.
- How well we treated people.

This list is by no means complete. Still, the list of things that may not be important in the end is equally significant. Many people spend most of their lives focusing on those things, only to have regrets at the end. The following list could give an idea of some things that might not matter in the end. They include the following:

- Your appearance—what you looked like or what you did to look the way you did.
- Where you are from.
- Where you lived or the place in which you live now.

What Matters in the End?

- Your level of intelligence and education, where you went to school and whether you did.
- The amount of money you made.
- The amount of money that you have in the bank.
- How much property you own and the types of property that you own.
- The quality and the value of the things that you own.
- The types and the number of vehicles that you owned and what you drive.
- How well-traveled you were and how you traveled.
- Your profession, the type of job you have, or how you made a living.
- The clubs, groups, or other organizations to which you belonged.
- The kinds of clothes you wore or where you shopped.
- Your perceived status in life.
- How much you know.
- What skills you possessed.
- The kinds of friends you had and how many.
- How crafty you were.

In the final analysis, there is one very important thing on which we could all agree. Human beings have consistently demonstrated their capacity to evolve, to adapt, and to survive. Throughout our history, we have learned numerous lessons, and by paying attention to them, our continued survival has been successfully guaranteed. What is also true, is that although we know so much about our survival as a species and about living, there remains a great deal that we do not know about life itself.

What appears abundantly clear, also, is that no matter how long we live, the questions to which we have failed to find answers, will continue to remain unanswered. Maybe, simple as they seem, they are beyond our human comprehension. Maybe, for those who believe life is transitional but continuous, the answers that they so desperately seek, may be revealed after their transition. Or maybe, it is just all hopeful and speculative, and this is it. Who knows? In the end, your guess, and your belief, may be just as good as mine.

I truly enjoyed putting this small volume together. As I wrote and as I reflected on my own life, many other questions were generated that I had never even thought of before. It is my wish that you, the reader, also found yourself thinking about other things that may matter to

What Matters in the End?

you in the end. Perhaps, even more importantly, I hope this will all enable you to arrive at a place where you find your own answers to many of the questions that your humble servant simply could not. Whatever position you choose to take, and wherever you finally end up, I hope it is at a desirable place, and one much better than this. Indeed, I hope that you will find peace.

We must approach the future with a great deal of hope. We have no other choice. It is my hope also, that in seeking the answers to your own questions, you will get the opportunity to recognize that even with your perceived insignificance in this very vast universe, your existence does matter. You are very much a part of this universe, and without you in it, it would just not be the same.

I hope you find out who you are. I hope you uncover your purpose in this very short but extremely important life, and if you haven't done so yet, I hope you figure out the role that your parents played in all of it. Even if your life is not as perfect as you wished it might have been, I hope you find at least aspects of it fulfilling. I hope that at some point, you will come to the realization that in the grand scheme of things, you may never find answers to the burning questions that you and so many others have always sought, and I hope you will be okay with that.

Finally, I hope you come to realize, that just like billions before you, no matter how long you live, much of your life will remain incomprehensible to you. Yet, in the end, if you find time to reflect, you may at least be more inclined to accept the possibility that on some level, it all did matter and it still does matter. We all do matter. We absolutely do!

Final Thoughts

IN RECENT YEARS, the advent of significant events on our planet has disturbed our peace of mind and we have lost many of our loved ones. Among those events are the worsening global warming situation (which some individuals are simply not taking as seriously as they should), the COVID-19 pandemic, and the most recent Russia-Ukraine war.

These events are all unprecedented. Yet, owing to the number of people who have been displaced in such a short time, the wanton loss of so many lives, and the use of buzzwords like nuclear weapons, in an already nervous and depressed world, are resulting in behaviors among human beings that are just extraordinary. Indeed, the current situations have many individuals reassessing their lives and taking a closer look at how they have been living. In many cases, they are even wondering whether we might indeed be approaching the end, and whether we may be on the verge of destroying ourselves.

There has never been a time in my six decades of life or during my twenty-five years of counseling, that I have ever dealt with as many cases in which there is so much concern. One just needs to put on the evening news, and there is usually so much negative information being disseminated that even the strongest among us may not want to be kept informed.

Current data suggest that many relationships are collapsing, that incidents of domestic violence and abuse are on the rise, that addictive behaviors are increasing, as are the rates of anxiety, depression, and even suicide. These increases point to a corresponding rise in several mental health conditions that are of significance, and to the understanding that there are ample reasons to be concerned. They leave many individuals thinking about our survival as a species, and what the outcome will eventually be.

As the demand for much needed mental health services increases, for the first time, many of my colleagues including myself have long waiting lists for individuals who are seeking counseling. Some counselors are also concerned that if they continue to work at the current pace without investing more heavily in their own self-care, they could see the possibility of burnout occurring.

The harsh reality is that there has been a dire shortage of trained mental health personnel for quite some time. The rate at which new therapists have been entering

Final Thoughts

the field, has been totally disproportionate to the ever increasingly high demand for services. The result is that many individuals have become very discouraged, unmotivated, and even more depressed. They need assistance, they developed the courage to ask for help, but they simply do not know where else to turn. Clearly, this is an area that merits a great deal more attention than it has been receiving.

Additionally, there are concerns regarding the mental health of many medical and allied health practitioners including mental health service providers as well. We must not forget that they are humans also, and they have also been experiencing many of the same challenges as the patients with whom they work. Just like everyone else, they have families, they are exposed to the same stressors, they are at risk of getting the same illnesses, and, if they do not seize the opportunity to care for themselves, they may not be able to help others very effectively.

The bottom line is that life on the planet has changed significantly in recent times, for all of us. We are dealing with far more uncertainty than we did before, and we find ourselves grappling with even more anxiety. Yet, getting into a state of panic will not help any of us. To survive, and we will, we must find ways to preserve our peace of mind.

Now is the time for more self-analysis. We must take a closer look at how we are living our lives. We must make desirable changes as they become necessary, and no matter how much things change, we must never allow ourselves to lose hope.

Let's face it; even after all this time, there are many things that we still do not know or understand about ourselves as a species. Even so, we do have a significant amount of knowledge that we can use to our benefit. Surely, we must reiterate that we may not understand who we really are, why we are here, what our purpose is, whether we are living fulfilling lives, or what matters in the end.

What we do know, however, is that we are here, our presence matters, and there are always steps that we can take to make our existence seem more worthwhile. We should all strive to do things that are good and that are harmonious with the universe. By doing so, it could help us preserve ourselves and our species. And, who knows? Perhaps in the process, we might even be able to find at least some of the answers to the burning questions that we have had for so long.

References

Baker, Amy J. L. 2007. *Adult Children of Parental Alienation Syndrome.* New York: Norton & Company. www.amyjlbaker.com

Centers for Disease Control and Prevention, Atlanta, Georgia : cdc.gov

Father Facts 8th Edition : National Fatherhood Initiative: www.fatherhood.org

United States Census Bureau: www.census.gov

Fulfilled

Important Hotline Numbers

American Counseling Association   1-800-347-6647

American Psychological Association   1-800374-2721

Crisis Call Center   1-800-273-8255

National Institute of Mental Health   1-301-443-4513

Substance Abuse & Mental Health Services
Administration   1-800-662-4357

Suicide Prevention   1-800-273-8255

www.ingramcontent.com/pod-product-compliance
Lightning Source LLC
Chambersburg PA
CBHW031258110426
42743CB00040B/727